Windows
on the Word

Windows on the Word

Useable Illustrations for Any Occasion

Dennis J. DeHaan, *Compiler*

BAKER BOOK HOUSE
Grand Rapids, Michigan 49506

ISBN: 0-8010-2946-5

Printed in the United States of America

Cover photo by Michael Forrest

Contents

Preface

The telling of a tale, the relating of an incident, whether true or fictitious, captures the imagination and stirs the heart as few other forms of discourse. Stories have always been loved—by all ages, in all ages. Even stories worn thin with the retelling seldom wear out. One illustration is worth a thousand words, and seems to have as much impact as page upon page of the most well-written prose.

From its beginning in 1956, *Our Daily Bread* has used the interest-holding power of anecdotes, incidents, and illustrations to drive home and reinforce the spiritual truths of the Bible. Stories have served as *windows on the Word,* letting light into the mind to help illumine scriptural truth.

This volume is a collection of some of the more appealing stories from *Our Daily Bread.* To the longtime reader of the devotional booklet, they will seem like old acquaintances dropping in for a brief but friendly visit. Many are true-life accounts. Others are fictitious, but they make a strong point. Some are quotes from gifted preachers; others are striking facts that underscore a timeless truth in a unique and interesting way.

Windows on the Word will be welcomed by pastors, teachers, and speakers, who are always on the lookout for good illustrations, but it is designed primarily for the blessing and encouragement of Christians in general. Unlike the devotional articles from which the stories are taken, each item makes its own point with little or no application. A biblical text appears before each entry, and the reader will readily see the vital relationship between the two. Reading the story and the text will provide a window on the Word, letting the Holy Spirit illumine the truth by way of illustration, application, or explanation.

The book is arranged alphabetically according to categories. The choice of topics is somewhat arbitrary, covering subjects that appear most often in the devotional guide, and they relate to the basics of the Christian life. Because *Our Daily Bread* has an evangelistic as well as a devotional purpose, a grouping on salvation has been included. The material in this book was selected from the 1970 through 1983 editions of *Our Daily Bread*.

To give the book added usefulness to those who are interested in a topical study, a section entitled "For Further Study" appears at the end of each category. The Scriptures listed under this heading relate to the broad subject under which the items appear—not necessarily to individual stories. These references are not included in the scriptural index.

Our earnest prayer is that *Windows on the Word* will make God's truth relevant to daily living. Many people have been introduced to the Scriptures through reading *Our Daily Bread*. We hope that these stories and incidents, reprinted in a different setting, will open our eyes to new light on God's Word. It is the Word that is "living, and powerful, and sharper than any two-edged sword" (Hebrews 4:12). It is the Word that "is profitable for doctrine, for reproof, for correction, for instruction in righteousness, that the man of God may be perfect, thoroughly furnished unto all good works" (2 Timothy 3:16,17).

Insofar as *Windows on the Word* helps to clarify for the reader what God is saying, it will serve the purpose for which it is sent forth.

—Dennis J. De Haan, Editor
Our Daily Bread

Anger

Wrath is cruel, and anger is outrageous.
Proverbs 27:4

A woman approached Billy Sunday and confessed that she had a very bad temper. She tried to cover up her sin by saying, "But Mr. Sunday, although I blow up over the least little thing, it's all over in a minute." The evangelist looked at her and then said, "So is a shotgun blast! It's over in seconds too, but look at the terrible damage it can do."

Be ye angry, and sin not; let not the sun go down
upon your wrath; neither give place to the devil.
Ephesians 4:26,27

When Leonardo da Vinci was painting "The Last Supper," he became incensed with a certain man. His temper flared, and he lashed out with bitter words. Turning again to his work, he attempted to brush some delicate lines onto the face of Jesus. But he was so distraught that he could not regain his composure. Unable to continue, he finally left his tools and went to look for the man and ask his forgiveness. Only after his apology was accepted and he was again right with God could Leonardo go back and complete the face of Christ.

But now ye also put off all these: anger, wrath,
malice, blasphemy, filthy communication out of
your mouth. *Colossians 3:8*

You have the most even temperament I have ever seen!" remarked one girl to another. "I don't see how you manage it." "Manage it?" echoed her friend. "I have to! I guess you don't know my family. In the little town where we lived, the children would run indoors when they saw my father coming down the street. And my grandfather in a wild fit of temper struck my grandmother, making her a helpless cripple. With a history like that, what could I expect but a life of insane rages? I determined by the grace of God I would not be like that. I went to Christ and prayed, 'Dear Lord, I know I can't handle my temper by myself. Please take control of my life for me.' And praise His name, He has!"

For Further Study: Job 5:2; Proverbs 22:24; Proverbs 27:3; Ecclesiastes 7:9; Mark 3:5; Galatians 5:16-26.

Assurance

These things have I written unto you that believe on the name of the Son of God, that ye may know that ye have eternal life, and that ye may believe on the name of the Son of God.   1 John 5:13

When George B. McClellan was commissioned Major General of the Army, he wrote his wife, "I don't feel any different than I did yesterday. Indeed, I have not yet put on my new uniform. I am sure that I am in command of the Union Army, however, because President Lincoln's order to that effect now lies before me." Accepting the authoritative word of his Commander in Chief, McClellan was confident of his position. Similarly, all who repent and receive Jesus Christ as Savior can completely trust God's Word, the Bible, which says that they are "justified by faith" (Rom. 5:1) and have "passed from death unto life" (1 John 3:14). When the Lord speaks, we can depend on what He says, for He cannot lie!

The Lord is my shepherd; I shall not want.
Psalm 23:1

An evangelist was staying with a couple whose young son was both deaf and mute. The guest asked God for wisdom to lead him to Christ. Since the youngster was just learning to read, the preacher thought he would write the first five words of the 23rd Psalm on the fingers of the boy's left hand. He would then go over the words by pointing to each finger. After repeating this for several days, he wrote a brief note telling him in simple terms that if he trusted Jesus as his Savior, the fourth word, "my," would become real to him and he could then be confident of going to heaven.

The evangelist's meetings in the town ended, and he had to leave before he was sure the boy fully understood the gospel invitation. Years later, however, he returned to the village and learned that the youngster became ill and had died shortly after his first visit. But just before he lapsed into unconsciousness, he had pointed to each of his five fingers. Then, with a smile on his face, he had gripped the fourth one. The preacher rejoiced, for the boy had testified the only way he could that he had truly placed his trust in Jesus.

We know that we have passed from death unto life, because we love the brethren. He that loveth not his brother abideth in death.   *1 John 3:14*

Writing about believers who are unsure of their salvation, Henry Bosch told of an aged woman who had accepted the Lord Jesus but was still plagued with doubts about her eternal destiny. So Henry's father and another elder were asked to counsel with her about her fears. After quoting several texts on assurance, one of them said, "Grandma, if you saw one group of people drinking, cursing, and singing worldly songs, and right next door a gathering of joyful believers was singing gospel hymns and testifying of God's saving grace, which company would attract you?" Without hesitation she exclaimed, "Oh, I'd only feel at home with the saints of God. I love to fellowship with them!" Then he showed her 1 John 3:14. As she read it, a happy smile brightened her face. By passing the "assurance test" given in that verse, she finally found peace.

For Further Study: Isaiah 32:17; Romans 8:16,17; 2 Timothy 1:12; 2 Timothy 4:18; Hebrews 10:22.

Atheism

The fool hath said in his heart, There is no God.
They are corrupt, they have done abominable
works, there is none that doeth good.　　*Psalm 14:1*

When D. L. Moody was conducting evangelistic meetings, he frequently faced hecklers who violently disagreed with him. In the final service of one campaign, an usher handed the famous preacher a note as he entered the auditorium. It was from an atheist who had been giving Mr. Moody a great deal of trouble. The evangelist, however, supposed that it was an announcement, so he quieted the large audience and prepared to read it. Opening the folded piece of paper, he found scrawled in large print only one word: "Fool!" The colorful preacher was equal to the occasion. Said Moody, "I've just been handed a memo which contains the single word—'Fool.' This is most unusual. I've often heard of people who write letters and forget to sign their names, but this is the first time I've ever heard of anyone who signed his name and then forgot to write the letter!" Taking advantage of the unique situation, Moody promptly changed his sermon text to Psalm 14:1, "The fool hath said in his heart, There is no God."

For the wrath of God is revealed from heaven
against all ungodliness and unrighteousness of
men, who hold the truth in unrighteousness,
because that which may be known of God is
manifest in them; for God hath shown it unto
them.　　*Romans 1:18,19*

In his book *The Case for Christianity*, C. S. Lewis said that when he was an atheist he rejected the idea of a

Divine Being because there was so much injustice in the world. The weakness of his argument became evident, however, when he asked himself, "But how had I gotten this idea of just and unjust? Man doesn't call a line crooked unless he has some idea of a straight line. What was I comparing this universe with when I called it unjust?" Of course, he could consider his idea of justice as nothing more than his own private notion. But this would destroy his case, for it depended on saying that there are real inequities in the world. So by denying the existence of God, he was saying, in effect, that everything is meaningless. Yet he had to assume that at least one part of reality does have meaning— his own idea of justice. Consequently, his atheism turned out to be too simple.

For Further Study: Exodus 3:14; 2 Kings 19:15; Job 12:7-25; Psalm 10:4; Isaiah 44:6; 1 Timothy 2:5; James 2:19.

Bible

Open Thou mine eyes, that I may behold wondrous things out of Thy law.　　　　*Psalm 119:18*

An elderly woman in Scotland was living in abject poverty. Many years earlier, her son had come to America and had not returned to his native land. One day a friend visited the mother and inquired, "Does your son ever help you with expenses?" Reluctantly she admitted, "No, but he writes me nice long letters and sends me interesting pictures." The visitor wanted to speak harshly of the man, but he held back and asked, "May I see the pictures?" The aged mother brought them out of a drawer, and to the friend's amazement they were valuable bank notes. Through the years she had been needlessly living in poverty.

But continue thou in the things which thou hast
learned and hast been assured of, knowing of
whom thou hast learned them, and that from a
child thou hast known the holy Scriptures, which
are able to make thee wise unto salvation through
faith which is in Christ Jesus.   2 Timothy 3:14,15

Four clergymen were discussing various Bible versions. One liked the King James because of its literary style. Another preferred the Revised Version of 1881, saying it gave the most literal rendering of the Hebrew and Greek. The third felt that Moffatt's was the most readable. The fourth minister remained silent. When they asked him for his opinion, he said, "I like my mother's translation best." The others were surprised and asked, "Did your mother translate the Bible?" "Oh, yes," he replied, "she translated it into life, and it was the most convincing version I ever saw."

I will delight myself in Thy statutes; I will not forget
Thy word.   Psalm 119:16

A small boy noticed a large black book covered with dust lying on a high shelf. His curiosity was aroused, so he asked his mother about it. Embarrassed, she hastily explained, "Oh, that's a Bible. That's God's Book." He thought for a moment, and then said, "Well, Mom, if that's God's Book, why don't we give it back to Him? Nobody around here uses it anyway!"

Search the Scriptures; for in them ye think ye have
eternal life; and they are they which testify of Me.
*   John 5:39*

One day in St. Louis, Missouri, a young convert named C. I. Scofield walked into the office of a friend. He found him with a new copy of the Scriptures on his desk and a pencil in his hand. "Why, man, you're spoiling that beautiful Bible!" exclaimed the young Christian. His older friend then pointed him to Acts 8, where he had underscored the fifth verse: "Then Philip went down to the city of Samaria, and preached Christ unto them." This he had connected by a line to the eighth verse, which reads, "And there was great joy in that city." Years afterward, Scofield frequently introduced his friend C. E. Paxson as "the man who first taught me to mark my Bible." The inspiration and instruction that Paxson gave him led to the preparation of the now-famous Scofield Reference Bible, with its helpful footnotes and cross-references.

Thy word have I hidden in mine heart, that I might not sin against Thee.   *Psalm 119:11*

Noted Bible teacher E. Schuyler English told about a Bible distributor, Michael Billester, who visited a small town in Poland shortly before World War II. Billester gave a Bible to a villager, who was converted by reading it. The new believer then passed the book on to others. The cycle of conversions and sharing continued until 200 people had become believers through that one Bible!

When Billester returned to Poland in 1940, this group of Christians met together for a worship service in which he was to preach the Word. He usually asked for testimonies, but this time he suggested that several in the audience recite verses of Scripture. One man stood and said, "Perhaps we have misunderstood. Did you mean verses or chapters?" These villagers had not memorized a few select verses of the Bible but whole chapters and books. Thirteen people knew Matthew, Luke, and half of Genesis. Another person had committed the entire book of Psalms to memory. That single copy of the Bible given by Billester had done its work. Transformed lives bore witness to the power of the Word.

*For the word of God is living, and powerful, and
sharper than any two-edged sword, piercing even to
the dividing asunder of soul and spirit, and of the
joints and marrow, and is a discerner of the
thoughts and intents of the heart.*   *Hebrews 4:12*

Many years ago something unusual happened in a
Moscow theater that illustrates the convicting and
transforming power of God's Word. Matinee idol
Alexander Rostovzev was converted while playing the
role of Jesus in a sacrilegious play entitled *Christ in a
Tuxedo*. He was supposed to read two verses from the
Sermon on the Mount, remove his gown, and cry out,
"Give me my tuxedo and top hat!" But as he read the
words, "Blessed are the poor in spirit; for theirs is the
kingdom of heaven. Blessed are they that mourn; for
they shall be comforted," he began to tremble. Instead
of following the script, he kept reading from Matthew
5, ignoring the coughs, calls, and foot-stamping of his
fellow actors. Finally, recalling a verse he had learned
in his childhood in a Russian Orthodox church, he
cried, "Lord, remember me when Thou comest into Thy
kingdom" (Luke 23:42). Before the curtain could be
lowered, Rostovzev had accepted Jesus Christ as his
personal Savior.

*But be ye doers of the word and not hearers only,
deceiving your own selves.*   *James 1:22*

One day a young Christian came into a mission
station in Korea to see the pastor who had been instrumental in his conversion. After the customary greet-
ings, the missionary asked the reason for his coming. "I
have been memorizing some verses in the Bible," he
said, "and I want to quote them to you." He had walked
hundreds of miles just to recite some Scripture verses
to his father in the faith. The pastor listened as he
repeated without error the entire Sermon on the
Mount. He commended the young man for his remarka-

ble feat of memory, then cautioned that he must not only "say" the Scriptures but also practice them. With glowing face, the man responded, "Oh, that is the way I learned them. I tried to memorize them, but they wouldn't stick. So I hit on this plan: First, I would learn a verse. Then I'd talk to a neighbor who was not a Christian and practice it on him. After doing this, I found I could remember it."

Then the devil taketh Him up into the holy city, and setteth Him on a pinnacle of the temple, and saith unto Him, If Thou be the Son of God, cast Thyself down; for it is written, He shall give His angels charge concerning Thee, and in their hands they shall bear Thee up, lest at any time Thou dash Thy foot against a stone. Matthew 4:5,6

A minister parked his car in a no parking zone in a large city. He was short of time and couldn't find a space with a meter. So he put a note under the windshield wiper, which read: "I have circled the block 10 times. I have an appointment to keep. *Forgive us our trespasses.*" When he returned, he found a citation from a police officer, along with this note: "I've circled this block for 10 years. If I don't give you a ticket, I lose my job. *Lead us not into temptation.*" The Word of God must never be used as a device to further our own purposes, to excuse a wrong, or to manipulate people.

Heaven and earth shall pass away, but My words shall not pass away. Matthew 24:35

A woman whose husband was an alcoholic led a most miserable life until someone gave her a Bible and she was converted. She found much comfort in reading it, and it became her most treasured possession. But her husband sneered at her newfound religion. One day he came home drunk, snatched the book from her hand,

and threw it into the fireplace. He shouted, "Now we'll see what will be left of your precious Bible!" But when he was cleaning out the ashes the next morning, he noticed a few pages that had not been burned. His eyes fell upon Jesus' words in Matthew 24:35, "Heaven and earth shall pass away, but *My words shall not pass away.*" He was startled as he paused to read that message. The Holy Spirit used this experience to convict him and bring saving faith to his soul.

For Further Study: Joshua 1:8; Psalm 19:7-14; Mark 12:24; 2 Timothy 3:16,17; 2 Peter 1:19-21; Revelation 22:19.

Christ

And the Word was made flesh, and dwelt among us (and we beheld His glory, the glory as of the only begotten of the Father), full of grace and truth.
                                          John 1:14

One of the great monarchs in Persia was known as a champion of the common people. To relate to their needs and problems, he would mingle with them in various disguises. On one occasion he went as a poor citizen to the public baths. In a tiny cellar he sat down beside the man who tended the furnace. He talked to the lonely fellow, and at mealtime he ate some of his plain food. In the weeks that followed, he visited him often and the man grew to love him dearly. Then one day the shah revealed his true identity. Expecting to hear a request for some expensive gift, he was surprised when his subject just sat there in silence, gazing at him in awe and astonishment. Finally he said respectfully, "You left your palace to sit with me in this dark place, to eat of my coarse bread, and to care whether my heart is glad or sad. You may give rich presents to others, but you have given yourself to me. Please, Your Majesty, never withdraw the priceless gift of your friendship."

For He is our peace, who hath made both [Jews and
Gentiles] one, and hath broken down the middle
wall of partition between us.   *Ephesians 2:14*

Many years ago the Prince of Wales visited the capital city of India. A formidable barrier had been set up to keep back the masses of people who wanted to catch a glimpse of royalty. When the prince arrived, he shook hands with some of the political dignitaries who were presented to him. Then, looking over their heads to the crowds beyond, he said, "Take down those barriers!" They were quickly removed, and the people, regardless of social rank, had free access to the heir to the British throne. Some time later when the prince came to that district again, 10,000 outcasts waited under a banner inscribed with these words: "The Prince of the Outcasts."

Now, when the centurion, and they that were with
him watching Jesus, saw the earthquake, and those
things that were done, they feared greatly, saying,
Truly, this was the Son of God.   *Matthew 27:54*

The following incident is related by David James Burrell: "Two agnostics were discussing the life of Jesus of Nazareth. One of them said, 'I think an interesting romance could be written about Him.' The other replied, 'And you're just the man to write it. First set forth the fundamentalist view that Christ is divine. Then tear down that prevailing sentiment and portray Him as He was—a *man* among men.' The advice was acted upon and the book was written. The person who made the suggestion was Colonel Robert Ingersoll; the author was General Lew Wallace; and the novel was *Ben-Hur.* In the process of his research, Wallace found himself confronted by the unique Man of the Scriptures. The more he studied His life and character, the more profoundly he was convinced that Jesus was divine. Finally, like the centurion beside the cross, he was constrained to cry, 'Truly, this was the Son of God.' "

21

He came unto His own, and His own received
Him not.   *John 1:11*

A story in *The King's Business* magazine told of a Christian fisherman who heard a loud splash one night as he lay in his boat. He knew that the man in the yacht nearby had been drinking heavily, so without hesitation he jumped into the cold water and with great effort succeeded in pulling the half-drowned victim back on board. He gave him artificial respiration, and then put him in his berth. Having done what he could to make him comfortable, he swam back to his own boat. The next morning he returned to the yacht to see how the man was doing. "It's none of your business!" said the man defensively. The fisherman reminded him that he had risked his life to save him. But instead of showing gratitude, the other fellow openly cursed him. As the Christian rowed away, tears filled his eyes. Looking up to heaven, he prayed, "When I think of how men have treated You, dear Lord, I'm filled with sorrow. Now I can begin to understand just a little how You must feel."

For Further Study: Matthew 1:18-25; John 8:58; John 10:30-33; Colossians 1:15-19; Hebrews 1:1-4; 1 John 5:20.

Church

And I say also unto thee, That thou art Peter, and
upon this rock I will build My church, and the gates
of hades shall not prevail against it.   *Matthew 16:18*

A story related by C. H. Spurgeon tells how the church of Jesus Christ withstands the power of those who hate it and would try to wipe it off the face of the earth. He wrote, "A medal was struck by Diocletian (cruel emperor of Rome) which still remains, bearing the inscription, 'The name of Christians being extinguished.' And in Spain, two monuments were raised. On one was written: 'Diocletian, for having extended the Roman Empire in the east and west, and for having extinguished the name of Christians, who brought the Republic to ruin.' On the other was inscribed, 'Diocletian, for having everywhere abolished the superstition of Christ, for having extended the worship of the gods.' As a modern writer has observed, 'We have here a monument raised by paganism over the grave of its vanquished foe. But far from being deceased, Christianity was on the eve of its final and permanent triumph. Neither in Spain, nor elsewhere, can be pointed out the burial place of Christianity; it is not, for the living have no tomb."

For by one Spirit were we all baptized into one body, whether we be Jews or Greeks, whether we be bond or free; and have been all made to drink into one Spirit.   *1 Corinthians 12:13*

The story is told about the members of a congregation who got into a squabble over the issue of predestination and free will. As the controversy raged, the people separated, going to opposite sides of the auditorium. One man did not know which group to join, so he slipped into the predestination crowd—but he didn't stay long. Someone asked him, "Who sent you here?" He replied, "No one, I came of my own free will." This brought the angry response, "What? You can't be one of us and talk that way." Quickly he was shoved across the aisle. But now he was questioned about his reasons for joining the freewill group. When he said, "I was forced over here," they indignantly shouted, "Get out! You can't join us unless you choose to do so." This poor believer was shut out from his brothers and sisters in Christ because they were fighting over a problem that's beyond the full grasp of man's puny little mind.

*There is neither Jew nor Greek, there is neither
bond nor free, there is neither male nor female; for
ye are all one in Christ Jesus.*   *Galatians 3:28*

A missionary who served in Calcutta said that she
was profoundly influenced because of a communion
service she had attended during the Second World
War. The leader of that meeting was a Swedish
minister. Among those present were a Chinese pastor,
a Japanese teacher, a German doctor, several English
citizens, and a small group of Indian believers. The missionary recalled that as she looked at that diverse
company she felt a closeness to each person, especially
when they partook of the bread and the cup. The bond
of Christian fellowship was real, even though some of
those people were from countries engaged in a brutal
war. Yes, Jesus Christ does remove the barriers of race
and nationality, and He takes away the hatreds that so
often spring from these differences.

For Further Study: Ephesians 4:1-16; Ephesians 5:23;
Colossians 1:18; 1 Timothy 3:15.

Comfort

*Blessed be God, even the Father of our Lord Jesus
Christ, the Father of mercies, and the God of all
comfort, who comforteth us in all our tribulation,
that we may be able to comfort them who are in any
trouble, by the comfort with which we ourselves are
comforted of God.*   *2 Corinthians 1:3,4*

One day Commissioner Frederick Booth-Tucker of
the Salvation Army was preaching in Chicago when a
man stepped out of the crowd and said to him before the
entire audience, "Booth-Tucker, you can talk about
how Christ is dear to you; but if your wife were dead, as
my wife is, and you had babies crying for their mother,

you couldn't say what you are saying." A few days later, Booth-Tucker lost his lovely wife in a tragic train accident. Her body was returned to Chicago for the funeral. As the service concluded, the husband took his place by the casket and said, "The other day when I was preaching in this city, a man said that if my wife were dead and my children were crying for their mother, I couldn't say Christ was sufficient. If that man is here, I tell him Christ *is* sufficient! My heart is crushed, bleeding, and broken. But there is a song in my heart, and Christ put it there. The Savior speaks comfort to me today." The man was present, and on hearing that, he came down the aisle to surrender his life to the Lord.

For Further Study: Psalm 77; 2 Corinthians 7:6-13; 1 Thessalonians 3:6-8.

Conscience

The wicked flee when no man pursueth, but the
righteous are bold as a lion.　　　　　*Proverbs 28:1*

A farmer was on his way home after picking up his new car. As he approached his farm, he decided to test the acceleration. He raced by the side road that led to his house and drove on for a mile or so. Then, after making a sharp U-turn, he sped back toward the side road. A man driving a station wagon observed the U-turn and the farmer's fast rate of speed, and he thought the automobile was an unmarked police car. Trying to avoid detection, he quickly headed down the road leading to the farm. Of course, he was followed by the returning farmer, who only wanted to go home. The second driver was alarmed and drove at high speed to escape, only to come to a dead end. He jumped out and ran, abandoning the station wagon. Later it was found to be filled with stolen coffee, cigarettes, and ammunition. His conscience had made him flee, even though no one was pursuing him.

*And in this do I exercise myself, to have always a
conscience void of offense toward God, and toward
men.*   Acts 24:16

One night a little boy was saying his bedtime
prayers with his grandmother. As he came to the
words, "If I should die before I wake," his voice trailed
off. Suddenly he jumped to his feet and started
downstairs, calling out, "I'll be right back, Grandma."
A few minutes later he returned, dropped to his knees,
and began where he left off. When he was done, he explained to his puzzled grandmother, "I started to think
about dying. And I remembered that I had turned
Timmy's wooden soldiers on their heads so I could see
him get mad in the morning. But if I should die tonight,
I didn't want him to find that mess. So I had to go and
straighten 'em up." She smiled and said, "You did
right, my boy. I imagine that a good many people, if
they were honest, would have to interrupt their praying
to undo a wrong."

For Further Study: Psalm 32; Romans 2:12-16;
1 Corinthians 8; 1 Corinthians 10:23-33.

Contentment

*Fret not thyself because of evildoers, neither be thou
envious against the workers of iniquity.* Psalm 37:1

Many years ago George Gardiner was holding evangelistic meetings and God was blessing. At that time
his only income was from his speaking engagements.
With a wife and two children to support and several
unpaid bills, Gardiner was trusting God to meet his
needs. At the final service the leader announced that
the entire offering would be given to the guest as a love-
gift. The plates were passed, and the people gave
generously. After the meeting one of the ushers enthu-

siastically showed the speaker the total on the adding machine tape. But when the man in charge handed the guest preacher a check, it was for one-half of the offering.

Back at the motel, sleep eluded the evangelist's eyes. The hours passed—12 . . . 1 . . . 2 a.m. Exasperated, he finally reached for the Gideon Bible by his bedside and began reading where it fell open. The words of Psalm 37 struck him with full force: "Fret not thyself." "Trust in the Lord." "Evildoers shall be cut off." He set the Bible down and prayed, "Lord, what a fool I've been! Forgive me. Keep the other fellow awake—I'm going to get some sleep!" Victory had come, and in the weeks that followed, God provided the needed finances.

Let your manner of life be without covetousness, and be content with such things as ye have; for He hath said, I will never leave thee, nor forsake thee.
Hebrews 13:5

An ancient Persian legend tells of a wealthy man by the name of Al Haffed who owned a large farm. One evening a visitor related to him tales of fabulous amounts of diamonds that could be found in other parts of the world. He described the great riches they could bring him. The vision of all this wealth made Haffed feel poor by comparison. So, instead of caring for his own prosperous farm, he sold it and set out to find these treasures. But the search proved to be fruitless. Finally, penniless and in despair, he committed suicide by jumping into the sea. Meanwhile, the man who had purchased the farm noticed one day the glint of an unusual stone in a shallow stream on the property. He reached into the water, and to his amazement he pulled out a huge diamond. Later when working in his garden, he uncovered many more of the valuable gems. Poor Al Haffed had spent his life traveling to distant lands seeking jewels, when on the farm he had left behind were all the precious stones his heart could have ever desired.

*Not that I speak in respect of want; for I have
learned, in whatever state I am, in this to be
content.*   *Philippians 4:11*

A devout Quaker was leaning on his fence, watching a new neighbor move in next door. After all kinds of modern appliances, electronic gadgets, plush furniture, and costly wall hangings had been carried in, the onlooker called over, "If you find you're lacking anything, neighbor, let me know, and I'll show you how to live without it." That Quaker had learned the secret of contentment.

*And having food and raiment let us be therewith
content.*   *1 Timothy 6:8*

One day Lord Congleton, a godly man, overheard one of his kitchen servants remark, "Oh, if I only had 5 pounds, I would be perfectly content." Pondering her statement, he decided he would like to see someone who was perfectly content. So he went to the woman and said he had heard her remark and wanted to do something about it. He proceeded to give her a 5-pound note. With great feeling, she thanked him for his generosity. Congleton then left the kitchen, but paused for a moment outside the door. As soon as the woman thought he was gone, she began to complain, "Why on earth didn't I say 10 pounds!"

For Further Study: Psalm 16:6; Proverbs 30:8;
Ecclesiastes 4:6; Galatians 5:26; 1 Timothy 6:6,7.

Courage

*Unto Thee will I cry, O Lord, my rock; be not silent
to me, lest, if Thou be silent to me, I become like
those who go down into the pit.*   *Psalm 28:1*

Frederick the Great, King of Prussia, invited some notable people to his royal table, including his top-ranking generals. One of them by the name of Hans von Zieten declined the invitation because he wanted to partake of communion at his church. Some time later at another banquet, Frederick and his guests mocked the general for his religious scruples and made jokes about the Lord's Supper. In great peril of his life, the officer stood to his feet and said respectfully to the monarch, "My lord, there is a greater King than you, a King to whom I have sworn allegiance even unto death. I am a Christian man, and I cannot sit quietly as the Lord's name is dishonored, His character belittled, and His cause subjected to ridicule. With your permission I shall withdraw." The other generals trembled in silence, knowing that von Zieten might be killed. But to their surprise, Frederick grasped the hand of this courageous man, asked his forgiveness, and requested that he remain. He promised that he would never again allow such a travesty to be made of sacred things.

Wait on the Lord; be of good courage, and He shall strengthen thine heart. Wait, I say, on the Lord.
Psalm 27:14

When the English steamer *Stella* was wrecked on the Casquet Rocks, a lifeboat with 12 women was lowered into the water. The storm quickly whirled them away and over the turbulent waves without a sailor aboard to steer and without an oar for them to use. They could only sit still and let the winds drive the craft aimlessly through the breakers. Cold and wet, the women spent a terrible night and would have lost courage had it not been for Margaret Williams. This Christian lady was well-known for her musical talent in sacred oratorios. A person of great spiritual stamina, she kept singing one song after another to her companions. All through the night her voice rang out over the waters. In addition to numerous hymns, she sang selections from the *Messiah* and the *Elijah*. Inspired by these stirring renditions, the women remained confident that God would bring them deliverance. Early the next morning, while it was still dark, a rescue boat came across the waters looking for survivors. It would have passed them by if the men had not heard Miss Williams' strong voice at just that moment, singing, "Oh, rest in the Lord, wait patiently for Him." Steering in the direction of the song, the rescuers were able to save the 12 women.

Then spoke the Lord to Paul in the night by a vision,
Be not afraid, but speak, and hold not thy peace;
For I am with thee, and no man shall set on thee to
hurt thee; for I have many people in this city.
Acts 18:9,10

During his pastorate in Indianapolis, Henry Ward Beecher preached a series of sermons against gambling and the liquor trade, denouncing the men who profited by these evils. The *Gospel Herald* described his uncompromising stand when he was accosted on the street by a would-be assailant. Pistol in hand, the man demanded a retraction of the declarations he had made from the pulpit. "Take them back right now," he said with an oath, "or I'll shoot you on the spot!" "Shoot away!" was Beecher's response as he calmly walked on. After he had taken a few steps and nothing happened, he hurled over his shoulder this parting remark, "I don't believe you can hit the mark as well as I did!" Dumbfounded by Beecher's holy boldness, his enemy realized that this preacher could not be bluffed.

For Further Study: Joshua 1:6,9,18; Judges 7:7-23; Ezekiel 2:6; 1 Corinthians 16:13; 2 Timothy 1:7.

Creation

The heavens declare the glory of God, and the
firmament showeth His handiwork.   Psalm 19:1

Many years ago Sir Isaac Newton had someone build an exact replica of our solar system in miniature.

At its center was a large golden ball representing the sun, and revolving around it were smaller spheres attached at the ends of rods of varying lengths. They represented Mercury, Venus, Earth, Mars, and the other planets. These were all geared together by cogs and belts to make them move around the "sun."

As Newton was studying the model, a friend who did not believe in the biblical account of creation stopped by for a visit. Marveling at the device and watching as the scientist made the heavenly bodies move in their orbits, the man exclaimed, "My, Newton, what an exquisite thing! Who made it for you?" Without looking up, Sir Isaac replied, "Nobody." "Nobody?" his friend asked. "That's right! I said nobody! All of these balls and cogs and belts and gears just happened to come together, and wonder of wonders, by chance they began revolving in their set orbits and with perfect timing."

And God created great sea monsters, and every living creature that moveth, which the waters brought forth abundantly, after their kind, and every winged fowl after its kind: and God saw that it was good. Genesis 1:21

In a *Moody Monthly* article, Bob Devine pointed out several amazing facts about the great horned owl—facts that defy all possibility of an origin by chance. For one thing, these stately monarchs of the forest fly silently. Soft, downy feathers on the front of their wings keep them from being heard by the forest creatures that comprise their food supply. In addition, their eyes are 100 times more sensitive to light than those of humans, enabling them to see by starlight. Also, a horned owl's left ear is about an inch lower than his right ear. Because the sound waves from the left ear get to the brain a split-second faster than from the right, the brain can compute the source of the sound exactly. And owls have sound tunnels from their ears to their eyes. The saucer-shaped discs of feathers around the eyes serve as receivers (much like a dish antenna) to collect sound and transmit it to the brain. This helps the owl locate its prey before it flies silently down to capture it.

With these amazing characteristics, the great horned owl is able to survive in a hostile environment. Does he possess these traits by chance? Impossible! He's just one more reason to believe in God the Creator.

For Further Study: Genesis 1,2; Nehemiah 9:6; Acts 14:15; Hebrews 11:3.

Cross

But God commendeth His love toward us in that,
while we were yet sinners, Christ died for us.
Romans 5:8

During the war between Britain and France, men were conscripted into the French army by a lottery system. When someone's name was drawn, he had to go off to battle. But there was one exception: a person would be exempt if another were willing to take his place. On one occasion the authorities came to a man and told him he was among those who had been chosen. He refused to go, saying, "I was shot 2 years ago." At first they questioned his sanity, but he insisted that this was indeed the case. He claimed that the military records would show that he had been drafted 2 years earlier and that he had been killed in action. "How can that be?" they questioned. "You are alive now!" He explained that when his name came up, a close friend said to him, "You have a large family, but I am not married and nobody is dependent upon me. I'll take your name and address and go in your place." And that is indeed what the record showed. This unusual case was referred to Napoleon Bonaparte, who decided that the country had no legal claim on that man. He was free. He had died in the person of another!

And, being found in fashion as a man, He humbled
Himself and became obedient unto death, even
the death of the cross.   *Philippians 2:8*

Arthur Hutchinson, in his old novel *One Increasing
Purpose,* has a passage that speaks about the cross as a
declaration of God's love. He tells of the conversation
between a blind yeoman and an old furnituremaker. In
the story, the craftsman was trying to explain the
theory of his designs in furniture. He told the yeoman
that he believed he could express himself best through
his craft. "Artists," he said, "express themselves in
colors, in words, in stone; well, I don't see why a man
can't express himself in wood." The yeoman, with
unusual spiritual insight, gave this surprising answer:
"In wood? It has been done, sir; yes, the mightiest expression of a man the world ever knew has been in
wood!" "What, yeoman?" asked the craftsman. "Sir,"
he answered, "the cross of Christ!"

Now is My soul troubled; and what shall I say?
Father, save Me from this hour. But for this cause
came I unto this hour.   *John 12:27*

The Birmingham City Art Gallery displays William
Hunt's famous picture *The Shadow of Death.* The artist
has portrayed Jesus as a youth in Joseph's carpenter
shop. The sun sinking in the western sky sends its
slanting rays through the open door. Jesus has gotten
up from His work and is stretching out His tired arms.
As He does, the setting sun casts a shadow on the wall
behind Him, creating the appearance of a man on a
cross.

I am the good shepherd; the good shepherd giveth
His life for the sheep.   *John 10:11*

A man named Jonas Brown once invited Bible expositor L. S. Bauman to stay in his home. Soon after the
preacher arrived in the farming community, an inci-

dent occurred which gave the man of God an opportunity to witness to his host. Writing about the experience, Bauman said, "One morning before breakfast, the farmer came to my room and beckoned me to follow him. He led me to one of the outer buildings where a hen sat on a nest with a brood of chickens peeking out from under her wings. 'Touch her,' Jonas said, 'she's stone dead! Look at that wound in her head. A weasel sucked all the blood from her body, and she never once moved, for fear the little beast would get her chicks.' Just a few days before, Jonas' wife had asked me to join her in praying for his conversion, and I had been hunting for some illustration to make plain to him the importance of the Savior's sacrifice. Now I saw my opportunity. 'Jonas,' I said, 'that was just like Christ. He endured all that suffering on the cross on behalf of us sinners. He could have moved but He wouldn't, because you and I were under His wings. If He had saved Himself, we would have been lost.' The Lord used those simple comments to convict that farmer of his need. A few more words from the Scripture and Jonas, enlightened by the Holy Spirit, knelt on the floor of the henhouse and gave his heart to Christ."

For Further Study: Matthew 27; 1 Corinthians 1:17,18; Galatians 3:13,14; Colossians 1:19,20; Hebrews 12:1,2.

Death

Therefore, we are always confident, knowing that, while we are at home in the body, we are absent from the Lord (for we walk by faith, not by sight); we are confident, I say, and willing rather to be absent from the body, and to be present with the Lord.   2 Corinthians 5:6-8

In his book *The Best Is Yet to Be,* Henry Durbanville told of an elderly lady who lived in southwest Scotland. She wanted very much to see the city of Edinburgh, but she was afraid to take the train because it had to go through a long tunnel to get there. Circumstances arose one day that forced her to journey to Scotland's capital. She was filled with fear as the trip began, and her anxiety increased as the train sped along. Before the express reached the tunnel, however, the dear old soul, worn out with worry, fell fast asleep. When she awoke, she discovered that she was already in the city. The author commented, "It is even so with the dying saint. He closes his eyes on earth, passes into what he thinks of as the tunnel of death, and opens them immediately in the celestial land."

For here have we no continuing city, but we seek one to come.   *Hebrews 13:14*

Shortly before his death, Dr. M. R. De Haan, founder of Radio Bible Class, took great comfort from a little tract written by J. E. Campbell. It spoke of death in this rather unusual way: "Moving day is coming. Just when the van will stop at our home we do not know—but for everyone it is sure, and for those along in years it is soon. As the day approaches, we realize the necessity of leaving our present abode and occupying the new house 'not made with hands, eternal in the heavens.' Death for the believer is a Homegoing and not a dreaded parting. The Owner of the house I have occupied here on earth has served notice that I must soon move out. The foundation is crumbling, the heating system is failing, and the windows are getting dim."

Mark the perfect man, and behold the upright; for the end of that man is peace.   *Psalm 37:37*

Many years ago the ship known as the *Empress of Ireland* sank. Among its many passengers were 130 Salvation Army officers. Only 21 of those Christian workers' lives were spared—an unusually small number. Of the 109 who drowned, not one of them had a life preserver! Many of the survivors told how those

35

brave Christians, seeing that there were not enough lifebelts, took off their own and strapped them on to others, saying, "I know Jesus, so I can die better than you can!" Their supreme sacrifice and faithful words set a beautiful example which for many years inspired the Salvation Army to carry on courageously for God. Over the years, millions have come to recognize that born-again individuals can face death fearlessly.

Father, I will that they also, whom Thou hast given Me, be with Me where I am, that they may behold My glory, which Thou hast given Me; for Thou lovedst Me before the foundation of the world.
John 17:24

Ida M. Clark was overwhelmed with grief as she went to her church on the Sunday morning after her mother had died. Just before she reached the door, a 7-year-old boy met her. He stopped, planted his feet solidly on the path in front of her, and with tearful eyes looked up at her. "I prayed for your mother," he said, "but she died." For a moment the sorrowing woman wanted to scoop him up in her arms and cry with him, but she could see he was seriously disturbed because he thought his prayers had not been answered. So she quickly and quietly lifted her heart in a silent petition, "O Lord, give me the right answer." Solemnly she said to the boy, "You wanted God to do His best for my mother, didn't you?" He nodded slowly. "Son, He answered your prayer. His best for her was to take her home to live with Him." The lad's eyes brightened as he replied, "That's right, He did." Then off he ran to meet his friends, content that God had taken her to heaven. And Ida Clark's own sorrow was comforted.

For His anger endureth but a moment; in His favor is life. Weeping may endure for a night, but joy cometh in the morning.
Psalm 30:5

As a young man, Henry Bosch worked during the summer months with his father, who was superintendent of the Garfield Park Cemetery in Grand Rapids. During that time Henry observed many graveside services. But the one that was held for the little daughter of a minister had a lasting effect on him. The pastor and his wife had prayed for a child for many years and finally were blessed with a beautiful baby girl. They were overjoyed with this treasured gift from the Lord. Then, at about the age of 6, a tragic accident took her life. After the funeral in their church, the public was allowed to attend the committal service. A large crowd had gathered, and the coffin was opened once more for the benefit of many friends. Even in death, the child was a picture of loveliness, with her long curls cascading down her shoulders. As the parents stood gazing at her lifeless form, a calm confidence could be seen in their faces. Then the father raised his hand heavenward and with tears rolling down his cheeks said, "Goodnight, darling, we'll meet you in heaven. We loved you so much, but Jesus loved you more. Goodnight." Not a dry eye could be seen! That godly pastor and his wife lived in the hope of the resurrection. They knew that "weeping may endure for a night, but joy cometh in the morning."

O death, where is thy sting? O grave, where is thy victory? The sting of death is sin; and the strength of sin is the law. 1 Corinthians 15:55,56

Many years ago, Dr. M. R. De Haan was walking in a field with his two young sons when a bee from one of his hives made a beeline for Richard and stung him just above the eye. He quickly brushed it away and threw himself in the grass, kicking and screaming for help. Then the bee went straight for Marvin and began buzzing around his head. The next thing Dr. De Haan knew, Marvin was also lying in the grass, yelling at the top of his lungs. But his dad picked him up and told him to stop crying. "That bee is harmless," Dr. De Haan assured him. "It can't hurt you. It has lost its sting." Then he took the frightened lad over to his elder brother, showed him the little black stinger in his brow, and said, "The bee can still scare you, but it is powerless to hurt you. Your brother took the sting away by being stung." Then he explained 1 Corinthians 15:56 by telling them that the sting of death is sin, and that Christ has borne its penalty for us on Calvary's cross.

For Further Study: Psalm 16:9-11; Proverbs 14:32; Luke 16:19-31; Romans 8:18; Ephesians 4:8-10; Philippians 1:21-23.

Discipleship

And he that taketh not his cross and followeth after Me, is not worthy of Me. He that findeth his life shall lose it; and he that loseth his life for My sake shall find it.   *Matthew 10:38,39*

In his book *Remember All the Way,* William C. Townsend related the story of an evangelist who felt like resigning from his task because he had run into problems and criticisms. He said to a colleague, "Don Guillermo, I'm going to quit." "Why are you giving your resignation to me?" Guillermo replied. "When you began your service, you said the Lord Jesus Christ was calling you to tell others about Him. I think you'd better present your resignation to the One who called you. Let's get down on our knees here, and you tell Him that you are going to quit. Let Him hear what you've just told me—that it's too hard, that too many people criticize you. Tell the Lord what you wanted to tell me. He's the One who sent you." "Well, I hesitate to do that," he replied. "I'm afraid He'll tell me to stay with the job." Don Guillermo then said pointedly, "If that's what He wants, don't you think you'd better stay?" "Yes, I think I should!" Taking new courage and refusing to look back, the evangelist went on to plow a straight furrow for God.

Then said Jesus unto His disciples, If any man will come after Me, let him deny himself, and take up his cross, and follow Me.   *Matthew 16:24*

An ocean-going ship was caught in the throes of a raging storm. It lost its power and began taking on water. Recognizing the peril facing the crew and himself, the captain sent out an SOS. The distress signal was picked up by the skipper of a vessel in a nearby harbor. Without hesitation he and his men made ready to take up the search. The storm worsened as they left port, and it looked like their mission of mercy might be thwarted. One of the crew on the rescue ship was stricken with fear. He rushed to the captain and shouted, "Turn around! Turn around! If we go any farther, we'll never come back!" The commanding officer replied, "Turn around? Did you say turn around? Never! Our obligation is to GO—not to come back!"

For My yoke is easy, and My burden is light.
Matthew 11:30

The noted preacher G. Campbell Morgan related this story: "A lady said to me some years ago, 'I'm tired of this worldly life. I'm going to give myself to Christ. I know what it means; I will have to do all the things I most dislike, but I am determined to be a real Christian.' When I returned to her town a year later, " said Morgan, "she was one of the first to welcome me. 'Do you recall,' she inquired, 'what I said to you when I rededicated my life?' I told her I certainly did. Then she looked at me, and the light of God was on her face as she exclaimed, 'But it's been so different, Dr. Morgan! When I began to follow Christ, I felt that I would have to do all the things that were contrary to my.desires. But now I do what I want every day, because God has made me pleased with the things that please Him!' "

For Further Study: Matthew 10:32-39; Luke 14:25-35; John 21:15-19.

Example

*Having your behavior honest among the Gentiles,
that, whereas they speak against you as evildoers,
they may by your good works, which they shall
behold, glorify God in the day of visitation.*

1 Peter 2:12

The importance of living a Christlike life is illustrated in a story from a book by Leslie B. Flynn, *Dare to Care Like Jesus*. He wrote, "A Christian baroness, living in the highlands of Nairobi, Kenya, told of a young national who was employed as her houseboy. After 3 months he asked the baroness to give him a letter of reference to a friendly sheik some miles away. The baroness, not wishing the houseboy to leave just when he had learned the routine of the household, offered to increase his pay. The lad replied that he was not leaving for higher wages. Rather, he had decided that he would become either a Christian or a Muslim. This was why he had come to work for the baroness for 3 months. He had wished to see how Christians acted. Now he wanted to work for 3 months for the sheik to observe the ways of the Muslims. Then he would decide. The baroness was ashamed as she recalled the many shortcomings in her dealings with the houseboy. She could only exclaim, 'Why didn't you tell me at the beginning!'"

*Let your light so shine before men, that they may see
your good works, and glorify your Father, who is in
heaven.* *Matthew 5:16*

To convince the people of Philadelphia of the advantages of street lighting, Benjamin Franklin decided to show his neighbors how compelling a single light could be. He bought an attractive lantern, polished the glass, and placed it on a long bracket that extended from the front of his house. Each evening as darkness descended, he ignited the wick. His neighbors soon noticed the warm glow in front of his residence. Even those living farther away were attracted. Passersby found that the light helped them to avoid tripping over protruding stones in the roadway. Soon others placed lanterns in front of their homes, and eventually the city recognized the need for having well-lighted streets.

For Further Study: Nehemiah 5:8-19; Romans 15:2-7; Philippians 2:5-8; Philippians 4:8,9; 1 Peter 2:11-25.

Faith/Trust

O Thou my God, save Thy servant who trusteth in Thee.
Psalm 86:2

A group of botanists went on an expedition into a remote section in the Alps, searching for new varieties of flowers. As one of the scientists looked through his binoculars, he saw a beautiful, rare species growing at the bottom of a deep ravine. To reach it, someone would have to be lowered into that gorge. Noticing a local youngster standing nearby, the man asked him if he would help them get the flower. The boy was told that a rope would be tied around his waist and the men would then lower him to the floor of the canyon. Excited yet apprehensive about the adventure, the youngster peered thoughtfully into the chasm. "Wait," he said, "I'll be right back," and off he dashed. When he returned, he had a man with him. Then the boy said to the head botanist, "I'll go over the cliff now and get the flower for you, but this man must hold on to the rope. He's my dad!"

Commit thy way unto the Lord; trust also in Him, and He shall bring it to pass.
Psalm 37:5

V ance Havner told a story about an elderly lady who was greatly disturbed by her many troubles— both real and imaginary. Finally someone in her family tactfully told her, "Grandma, we've done all we

can for you. You'll just have to trust God for the rest."
A look of absolute despair spread over her face as she
replied, "Oh, dear, has it come to that?"

Enter into His gates with thanksgiving, and into His
courts with praise. Psalm 100:4

From the book *Their Finest Hour* by Charles Ludwig
comes this remarkable incident: "Charles A. Tindley, a
poverty-stricken black pastor, stood at desperation
corner. He was serving a tiny, struggling church in
Cape May, New Jersey, when a blizzard swept down,
paralyzing the town. During the cold, dark night his
baby died. Dawn brought no sign of relief. There was
nothing but stale bread for breakfast. . . . 'Set the table
like we always do,' he urged his wife. Courageously, he
thanked God for his salvation, his health, and his
children, confident that their needs would be met. As
the family listened in wonder, someone knocked on the
door. A brother in the Lord entered with his arms
loaded with groceries. The storm had delayed his
coming. Charles Tindley had passed a crucial test of
faith by remaining grateful under the darkest circumstances. This ex-slave went on to pastor a church
in Philadelphia that reached thousands, including a
grandson of the man who once owned him."

But without faith it is impossible to please Him; for
He that cometh to God must believe that He is, and
that He is a rewarder of them that diligently seek
Him. Hebrews 11:6

The *Sunday School Times* told the story of a minister
and his encounter with a banker. The man attended
the pastor's church only on rare occasions, but each
time the sermon was about the need for faith. On his
way out one morning the irritated banker finally said,
"Why don't you preach on something more practical!"
He was gone before the minister had a chance to

answer. A few days later, there was a run on this executive's bank, and many of the depositors were demanding their money. (This was in the days before "Uncle Sam" insured savings accounts.) The banker went up and down the line, reassuring them that their investments were perfectly safe. The pastor, who had come to see what was going on, inquired, "What's the problem?" "Nothing is actually wrong," he answered. "Everybody's just lost confidence in the bank because of some false rumors. If you can assure them that we're honest and their money is safe, I'd appreciate it." The preacher pondered a moment, then asked, "What about faith? Just recently you told me to preach on something more practical." "Yes, I remember it well, but I take it all back."

For Further Study: Jeremiah 17:7,8; Romans 1:16,17; Romans 4; Galatians 3; Hebrews 11; James 1.

Faithfulness

Fear none of those things which thou shalt suffer. Behold, the devil shall cast some of you into prison, that ye may be tried, and ye shall have tribulation ten days; be thou faithful unto death, and I will give thee a crown of life.　　　*Revelation 2:10*

One winter when the Roman emperor Licinius was persecuting the Christians, his Thundering Legion was stationed at Sebaste. Because 40 men in that company had declared themselves believers, they were sentenced to spend the night naked on a frozen pool. A large fire was kindled in a house nearby, and food and a warm bath were prepared for any who would renounce their faith. As daylight faded, 40 warriors continued to resist in spite of the bitter cold—some walking quickly to and fro, some already sleeping that sleep which ends in death, and some standing, lost in prayer. These words arose to heaven, "O Lord, 40 wrestlers have come forth to fight for Thee. Grant that 40 wrestlers may gain the victory!" Finally, one of them could endure the suffering no longer. He left the others and went into the house where Sempronius and his men were on guard. But still the petition went up from those able to speak, "O Lord, 40 wrestlers have come forth to fight for Thee. Grant that 40 wrestlers may gain the victory!" Their prayer was answered. Sempronius the centurion was touched by his comrades' bravery, and the Holy Spirit moved upon his heart. Declaring himself a Christian, he went to the frozen pond and took the place of the one defector. When the long night was over, 40 glorious spirits, Sempronius among them, had entered into the presence of Christ.

If we suffer, we shall also reign with Him; if we deny Him, He also will deny us.   *2 Timothy 2:12*

In the 17th century a girl named Maria Durant lived in southern France. She was attractive and intelligent, and life beckoned joyously to her. She was also deeply spiritual, and she was not ashamed to speak out for Christ. The persecution of Christians in that area, however, became so severe that her witness was no longer tolerated by the authorities. She refused to be silent and as a result was imprisoned. For 38 years, while life with its pleasures passed her by, she maintained a shining testimony. Her valiant stand for the truth was costly. Rather than yield to pressure and renounce her Lord, she stood firm. Knowing full well that her imprisonment was denying her the joys of marriage and a family, she would not compromise her faith. The years of privation finally sapped her strength, and she died a martyr's death. Maria Durant had not only lived a life of inward holiness, but she had also "resisted unto blood" the outward tide of iniquity. It is said that tourists still go and look with respect and sadness at the slogan scratched on the dungeon wall. It was this one word: RESIST!

Yet, if any man suffer as a Christian, let him not be
ashamed, but let him glorify God on this behalf.
1 Peter 4:16

In a magazine called *The Teacher*, Pastor Harold Dye wrote about an 8-year-old Mexican boy named Pedro. One Sunday, after hearing the minister preach on Simon of Cyrene, the lad came up to speak to him. "You asked what we'd do if we had been in the crowd when Jesus fell under the weight of His cross," said the youngster earnestly. "I'm sure I would have been happy to help carry it!" The boy had recently accepted Christ, although his parents were antagonistic to the gospel. To test him, the minister said, "Yes, but if you had helped the Lord, the cruel Roman soldiers would probably have beaten you with whips." Without hesitation, the boy answered, "I don't care! I love Him! I'd have done it just the same."

Two weeks later, Pastor Dye stood at the door of the church, greeting the people as they left the service. When Pedro came by, he patted him affectionately on his shoulder. Shrinking back with a little cry, the 8-year-old pleaded, "Please don't do that. My back is very sore." Since he had barely touched him, the minister was puzzled. He took the youngster to a nearby cloakroom and asked him to remove his shirt. Crisscrossing his back from his neck to his waist were huge red welts. "Who did that?" the preacher asked angrily. "My mother," said Pedro. "She whipped me because I came to church!" That Mexican boy proved he was willing to stand up for the One in whom he had put his trust.

For whosoever would save his life shall lose it; but
whosoever will lose his life for My sake, the same
shall save it.   *Luke 9:24*

John Huss, the Bohemian reformer, was burned at the stake in 1415. Before his accusers lit the fire, they placed on his head a paper crown with devils painted on it. He answered this mockery by saying, "Jesus Christ, my Lord, wore a crown of thorns for my sake; why should not I then, for His sake, wear this light crown, be it ever so ignominious? Truly I will do it willingly." After the wood was stacked up to Huss' neck, the Duke of Bavaria asked him to renounce his preaching. Trusting completely in God's Word, Huss replied, "In the truth of the gospel which I preached, I die willingly and joyfully today." The wood was ignited, and Huss died while singing, "Jesus Christ, the Son of the living God, have mercy on me."

Watch, stand fast in the faith, quit you like men, be strong.   *1 Corinthians 16:13*

George Whitefield, who lived about 200 years ago, exhibited an unflinching devotion to Christ. After preaching several times one day, he went to his room completely exhausted. As he was preparing for bed, he was informed that a large crowd had gathered and wanted him to speak just once more. Summoning his remaining strength, he took a candle with him and said he would preach till it was burned out. The taper flickered its last about an hour later, and Whitefield closed in prayer and went inside. The next morning they found him on his knees beside his bed—the flame of his earthly existence had glimmered and died. "Faithful unto death," he now awaits the promised crown!

Moreover, it is required in stewards, that a man be found faithful.   *1 Corinthians 4:2*

An elderly Scottish preacher was rebuked by one of his deacons one Sunday morning before the service. "Pastor," said the man, "something must be wrong with your preaching and your work. There's been only one person added to the church in a whole year, and he's just a boy." The minister listened, his eyes moistening and his thin hand trembling. "I feel it all," he replied, "but God knows I've tried to do my duty." On that day the minister's heart was heavy as he stood before his flock. As he finished the message, he felt a strong inclination to resign. After everyone else had left, that one boy came to him and asked, "Do you think if I worked hard for an education, I could become a preacher, or maybe a missionary?" Again tears welled up in the minister's eyes. "Ah, this heals the ache I feel," he said. "Robert, I see the Divine hand now. May God bless you, my boy. Yes, I think you will become a preacher."

Many years later an aged missionary returned to London from Africa. His name was spoken with reverence. Nobles invited him to their homes. Many souls had been added to the church of Jesus Christ, and he had reached even some of Africa's most savage chiefs. His name was Robert Moffat, the same Robert who years before had spoken to the pastor that Sunday morning in the old Scottish kirk.

For Further Study: 2 Samuel 22:22-25; Job 1:21,22; Daniel 1; Matthew 25:14-23.

Fear

When I am afraid, I will trust in Thee.　　Psalm 56:3

In his book *Three Deadly Foes,* Henry Durbanville wrote this about John Chrysostom: "Exiled from the position which he held as the greatest teacher of his age, this noble man refused to be intimidated. 'What can I fear?' Chrysostom asked. 'Will it be death? But you know that Christ is my life, and that I shall gain by death. Will it be exile? But the earth and all its fullness are the Lord's. Will it be loss of wealth? But we brought nothing into this world and can carry nothing out. Thus all the terrors of the world are contemptible in my eyes, and I smile at all its good things. Poverty I do not fear; riches I do not sigh for; and from death I do not shrink.' "

For Further Study: 1 Kings 17:13,14; Isaiah 41:10; Isaiah 43:1-3; Matthew 14:22-33; 2 Timothy 1:7.

Forgiveness

And be ye kind one to another, tenderhearted,
forgiving one another, even as God, for Christ's
sake, hath forgiven you.   *Ephesians 4:32*

Two missionaries in Korea discovered that they had violated the command of 1 Thessalonians 5:19, which says, "Quench not the Spirit." They had disagreed on a policy matter and had left a conference with bad feelings toward each other. But when they got back to their respective stations, neither had peace. Both sensed that something was wrong. Each felt a lack of power in his witness. Finally, one of them could stand it no longer, so he boarded a train and traveled 100 miles to see his fellow worker. When the two men met face to face, they embraced and both of them wept. Then, getting down on their knees, they asked God to forgive them and to rekindle their spiritual fervor. As a result, they returned to their labors with a new sense of the Holy Spirit's glow in their hearts. Moreover, the news of their reconciliation brought conviction to many believers who were at odds with one another. A wonderful revival followed and souls were won to Christ.

The discretion of a man deferreth his anger, and it
is his glory to pass over a transgression.
       Proverbs 19:11

Perhaps you've heard the story about the stubborn old farmer who was plowing his field. A neighbor who was watching as he tried to guide the mule finally said, "I don't want to butt in, but you could save yourself a lot of work by saying 'gee' and 'haw,' instead of jerking on the reins." The oldtimer mopped his brow and replied, "Yep, I know; but this here mule kicked me 6 years ago, and I ain't spoke to him since!"

Put on, therefore, as the elect of God, holy and
beloved, tender mercies, kindness, humbleness of
mind, meekness, longsuffering; forbearing one
another, and forgiving one another, if any man
have a quarrel against any; even as Christ forgave
you, so also do ye.   *Colossians 3:12,13*

A clerk was caught embezzling and was summoned
to the office of his employer, who was a Christian. The
least the man could expect was a blistering dismissal;
he might even be turned over to the police. When the
clerk entered the office, the older man spoke his name
and asked him if he was guilty. Shamefully, the employee stammered out, "Y-y-yes." The employer told
him he was not going to press charges, but then asked,
"If I take you back, can I trust you?" When the surprised but still remorseful clerk assured him that he
could be trusted, the employer continued. "You are the
second man who has fallen and has been pardoned in
this company," he said. "I was the first! I'm showing
you mercy, because I received mercy."

Then came Peter to Him, and said, Lord, how often
shall my brother sin against me, and I forgive him?
Till seven times? Jesus saith unto him, I say not
unto thee, Until seven times; but, Until seventy
times seven.   *Matthew 18:21,22*

Otto the Great, a 10th-century king of Germany,
once attended services at the cathedral of Frankfort.
As he entered, he was approached by an emaciated
man dressed in sackcloth. Pleading for mercy, his
hands raised in prayer, the poor penitent fell prostrate
at the monarch's feet. The monarch suddenly recognized that this was his own brother Henry, who years
before had severely wronged him. Remembering the ill
treatment and insults he had received at his hand, he

angrily pushed the former rebel out of the way with his foot. The religious services had already begun as he moved into the cathedral. Suddenly, as if the voice of God were speaking, he heard the minister read Matthew 18:21,22. Conscience-stricken, the emperor returned to where the repentant one lay sobbing. Raising him to his feet, he planted on his brow a fraternal kiss of brotherhood and pardon.

But I say unto you, Love your enemies, bless them that curse you, do good to them that hate you, and pray for them who despitefully use you, and persecute you.   *Matthew 5:44*

When Samuel Marsden went to Australia as a chaplain, he was assigned to minister to a group of convicts. Although many of the men were friendly, Marsden's earnest contending for the faith incurred the wrath of some who disliked his outspoken way of rebuking them for their sin. One afternoon while walking along a riverbank not far from his home, he saw an ex-convict jump into the river, apparently intending to commit suicide. Throwing off his coat, the chaplain plunged bravely into the swiftly flowing stream and sought to rescue him. To his horror he found that the man had merely decoyed him into the water to choke him and try to drown him. Eventually the rather tough and wiry Marsden exhausted his evil opponent and dragged him to the shore. Much to the surprise of the defeated one, Marsden invited him to his house, where he gave him dry clothing. The chaplain said, "I won't tell a soul what happened. I know God has already forgiven you, and so do I." The conscience-smitten man recognized that here indeed was one who practiced what he preached. He soon was led to Christ and later became a devoted assistant to the chaplain.

For Further Study: Genesis 33:1-16; Genesis 45:1-15; 1 Samuel 24; Luke 23:34; Philemon.

50

Giving

*He that hath pity upon the poor lendeth unto the
Lord, and that which he hath given will He pay him
again.*   *Proverbs 19:17*

When the British preacher C. H. Spurgeon went to
Bristol for the purpose of ministering there, he hoped
to collect 300 pounds to support his work with homeless
children in London. At the end of the week of meetings,
many people had been blessed, and his financial goal
had been reached. That night as he bowed in prayer,
Spurgeon seemed to hear a voice saying, "Give that
money to George Mueller." "Oh no, Lord," answered
the minister, "I need it for my own dear orphans." Yet
he couldn't shake the idea that God wanted him to part
with it. Only when he said, "Yes, Lord, I will," could he
find rest. Early the next morning he made his way to
Mueller's orphanage and found that great man of
prayer on his knees. The famous preacher placed his
hand on his shoulder and said, "George, God has told
me to give you this 300 pounds I've collected." "My
dear brother," said Mueller, "I've just been asking
Him for exactly that amount." The two servants of the
Lord then wept and rejoiced together. When Spurgeon
returned to London, he found a letter on his desk con-
taining 300 guineas. "There," he cried with joy, "the
Lord has returned my 300 pounds with 300 shillings
interest!"

*And there came a certain poor widow, and she
threw in two mites, which make a farthing.*
                                            Mark 12:42

A missionary told of a woman in India who was
holding a weak, whining infant in her arms, while at
her side stood a beautiful, healthy child. The man of
God saw her walk to the banks of the Ganges River and
throw the robust youngster to the crocodiles as an

offering, and then turn toward home again still clutching the sickly child to her bosom. Tears were running down her cheeks when he stopped to question her concerning her shocking actions. She proudly replied in defense of her conduct, "O sir, we always give our gods the best!"

Every man shall give as he is able, according to the blessing of the Lord thy God which He hath given thee.   *Deuteronomy 16:17*

A man knelt with his pastor and committed himself to God to give a certain percent of his income as long as he lived. From his first week's pay he gave $1 to the Lord. Soon his weekly offering had increased to $10. As time went on, he continued to prosper. Before long he was giving $100 a week, then $200, and in time, $500 a week. Finally he called the pastor. "Please come and see me," he said. "It's urgent!" When the minister arrived, the host said, "You remember that promise I made to God years ago? How can I get released? When I made the promise, all I had to give was a dollar, but now it's $500. I can't afford to give away money like that." The wise old pastor looked at his friend and said, "I'm afraid you cannot get a release from the promise, but there is something we can do. We can kneel down and ask God to shrink your income so that you can afford to give a dollar again."

The liberal soul shall be made fat, and he that watereth shall be watered also himself.
                          Proverbs 11:25

Shortly before the turn of the century, two young students were working their way through Stanford University. At one point their money was almost gone, so they decided to engage the great pianist Paderewski for a concert and use the profits for board and tuition. Paderewski's manager asked for a guarantee of $2,000. The students worked hard to promote the concert, but they came up $400 short. After the performance, they went to the musician, gave him all the money they had raised, and promised to pay the $400 as soon as they could. It appeared that their college days were over. "No, boys, that won't do," said the pianist. "Take out of this $1600 all your expenses, and keep for each of you 10 percent of the balance for your work. Let me have the rest."

Years passed. Paderewski became premier of Poland following World War I. Thousands of his countrymen were starving. Only one man could help—the head of the U.S. Food and Relief Bureau. Paderewski's appeal to him brought thousands of tons of food. Later he met the American statesman to thank him. "That's all right," replied Herbert Hoover. "Besides, you don't remember, but you helped me once when I was a student in college."

For Further Study: Proverbs 3:9,10; Malachi 3:10-12; Matthew 6:1-4; Matthew 25:34-40; 2 Corinthians 8:11-15; 2 Corinthians 9:6,7.

God's Care

But my God shall supply all your need according to His riches in glory by Christ Jesus.
Philippians 4:19

A seminary student and his wife had come to the end of their resources. They arrived at church one Sunday with only a nickel between them—in those days just enough for a loaf of day-old bread. The conscientious young man had a hard time parting with his last coin. But the moment he dropped it in the offering plate his heart was glad, for he knew God would provide. After the service a fellow Christian, who wasn't aware of his struggle, grasped his hand, spoke a word of encouragement, and gave him a 5-dollar bill! "Why did you do that?" asked the grateful student. The man replied, "The Lord seemed to whisper in my heart that you were in need. So please take the money as coming from Him!" God had supplied their need and honored their trust in Him. How that young couple rejoiced!

Are not two sparrows sold for a farthing? And one of them shall not fall on the ground without your Father.
                                                    Matthew 10:29

A magazine article told about a sparrow that had built its nest in a freight car, which was in the shop for repair. By the time it was ready for use, a family of young sparrows occupied a corner. The freight car traveled several hundred miles, and all the while the mother bird stayed with her young. The trainmen were touched by this scene and notified the division superintendent. He ordered that the boxcar be moved onto a siding and not used until the little birds were old enough to leave the nest and fly away. Think of it, a great railroad company going to such lengths to protect helpless little sparrows! Surely the Heavenly Father, who also cares for sparrows, will go to even greater lengths to guard His children!

And God is able to make all grace abound toward you, that ye, always having all sufficiency in all things, may abound to every good work.
                                                2 Corinthians 9:8

She was a woman with a cheerful disposition and a deep faith in God. That's how Henry Bosch described his Aunt Nellie who patiently attended her bedridden husband for 5 years. He was completely incapacitated, and she cared for him night and day until his death. The bills had mounted up, and she had no money to pay them. His insurance had lapsed, so the undertaker sympathetically agreed to wait for his fee. Through it all, Nellie was not depressed. When Henry visited her, she said, "God will supply my needs. I don't know how, but He will!" A few days later she received some wonderful news. A piece of land in Texas, purchased by her husband's father years before, had produced a small amount of oil. Soon a letter arrived with a check for more than $5,000 — her share of the earnings. It covered her expenses exactly — not a penny too little or a penny too much. What joy flooded her soul!

And we know that all things work together for good to them that love God.   *Romans 8:28*

The *Christian Victory* magazine tells of a missionary who was seriously ill at a foreign outpost. One month her check did not arrive, and she was forced to live day after day on oatmeal and canned milk. During those long days of illness and meager diet, she began to wonder if the Lord was neglecting her. After about 30 days of this restricted diet her symptoms disappeared, and she returned to good health. Not long after that, she got her check and was able to purchase some different food. When her furlough came, she told of her great trial to an eager audience. At the close of the meeting a kindly doctor asked about her ailment. When he heard the nature of her digestive malfunction, he said, "Well, if your check had arrived, you probably wouldn't be talking to me today. Because of what happened, your life was spared. You didn't know it, but what's usually prescribed for cases like yours is a 30-day oatmeal diet!" The woman then realized how wonderfully God had cared for her in her time of need.

The Lord is my strength and my shield; my heart trusted in Him, and I am helped. Therefore, my heart greatly rejoiceth, and with my song will I praise Him.   *Psalm 28:7*

The marvelous, providential care of God was deeply impressed upon gospel singer Ira D. Sankey many years ago. Traveling on a Delaware River steamer, he was recognized by some of the people on board. They had seen his picture in the newspaper and knew that he was associated with D. L. Moody, the evangelist. When he was asked to sing one of his own compositions, Sankey said he preferred the hymn by William Bradbury, "Savior, Like a Shepherd Lead Us." He suggested that everyone join with him in the singing. One of the stanzas begins, "We are Thine—do Thou befriend us, be the Guardian of our way." When he finished, a man stepped out of the shadows and inquired, "Were you in the Union Army, Mr. Sankey?" "Yes, I joined up in 1860." "Did you ever do guard duty at night in Maryland about 1862?" "Yes, I did." "Well, I was in the Confederate Army," said the stranger, "and I saw you one night at Sharpsburg. You were wearing your blue uniform, and I had you in my gunsight as you stood there in the light of the full moon. Just as I was about to pull the trigger, you began to sing." Sankey was astounded as he recalled the incident. "It was the same hymn you sang tonight," continued the man. "My mother often sang it, but I never expected to hear it at midnight by a soldier on guard duty. I realized you were a Christian, and I couldn't shoot you." Gratefully, Sankey embraced his former enemy.

Thou compasseth my path and my lying down, and art acquainted with all my ways.   **Psalm 139:3**

A little boy was eagerly looking forward to the birthday party of a friend who lived only a few blocks away. When the day finally arrived, a blizzard made the sidewalks and roads nearly impassable. The lad's father, sensing the danger, was reluctant to let his son go. The youngster reacted tearfully. "But Dad," he pleaded, "all the other kids will be there. Their parents are letting them go." The father thought for a moment, then replied softly, "All right, you may go." Surprised but overjoyed, the boy bundled up and plunged into the raging storm. The driving snow made visibility almost impossible, and it took him more than half an hour to trudge the short distance to the party. As he rang the doorbell, he turned to look out into the storm. His eye caught the shadow of a retreating figure. It was his father! He had followed his son's every step through the storm.

He delivereth me from mine enemies: yea, Thou
liftest me up above those who rise up against me.
Thou hast delivered me from the violent man.
                                        Psalm 18:48

While working among the Lebanese hill people called the Druse, a missionary named Gobat was invited by a village chief to visit him. Eager to witness to the non-Christian man, he accepted the invitation. On the day he was to go, however, he became ill and had to stay home. When a second invitation arrived, circumstances again interfered. Another summons came, and this time the missionary set out with a guide. But when a hyena crossed their path, the superstitious helper would go no farther and they had to return. Later Gobat learned that the village chief had an ulterior motive; he wanted to murder him! When that treacherous tribal leader heard of the obstacles, he exclaimed, "That missionary must be God's servant. I sent messenger after messenger to bring him, but he was always hindered."

Be merciful unto me, O God, be merciful unto me;
for my soul trusteth in Thee. Yea, in the shadow of
Thy wings will I make my refuge, until these
calamities be passed by.   *Psalm 57:1*

An experienced and capable pilot had been airborne only a few minutes in his private plane when both engines "conked out"! As he nosed down, hoping to find a place to land, a number of things suddenly flashed across his mind. He thought, "I'm gone, but sure of heaven. Better head for the river. Try to avoid hurting others when I crash. My wife will be displeased." The plane clipped some pine trees and then hit a high voltage line. Unknown to him, however, the power company a few months before had installed an automatic cutoff for that cable at the local substation. As a result, there was no current going through it at that moment. The line, acting like an arresting gear, slowed the plane and flipped it around. After dropping into an azalea bed, the airplane burned. But the man climbed out unscathed. A miraculous escape? It certainly was! This Christian pilot later testified, "I learned in those few moments that HE was in charge; there was nothing I could do."

God is in the midst of her; she shall not be moved.
God shall help her, and that right early.

Psalm 46:5

In 1346, during the Hundred Years War, the English army of King Edward III met a French battalion at Crecy, France. The king's son, Prince Edward, led one vital division of the British force, while Edward III stood nearby with a strong band of soldiers, ready to send relief if he saw the need. Soon after the battle started, the prince thought he was in danger, so he sent for help. But the king didn't come. So young Edward sent another message, pleading for immediate assistance. His father responded by telling the courier, "Go tell my son that I am not so inexperienced a commander as not to know when help is needed, nor so careless a father as not to send it."

My help cometh from the Lord, who made heaven
and earth.   *Psalm 121:2*

In the early days of the automobile, a man who was driving a Model-T had engine trouble. He couldn't get his car started, no matter how hard he turned the crank. He advanced the spark and tried to make some adjustments, but still it wouldn't run. Just then a chauffeured limousine pulled up. A wiry, energetic man stepped out from the back seat and offered his assistance. After tinkering under the hood a few moments, the stranger said, "Now try it!" Immediately the engine leaped to life. The well-dressed individual then identified himself as Henry Ford. "I designed and

built these cars," he said, "so I know what to do when
something goes wrong."

For Further Study: Psalm 23; Psalm 34:10; 2 Corinthians
1:3,4; 2 Corinthians 4:16-18; Philippians 4:6,7.

God's Leading

Wherefore, be ye not unwise but understanding
what the will of the Lord is.　　　　*Ephesians 5:17*

Perhaps you've heard of the man who wanted to
know God's will on a particular matter. He took his
Bible, opened it at random, and dropped his index
finger onto the page—assuming that the verse on
which it landed would tell him what to do. But much to
his chagrin, his finger fell on Matthew 27:5, which
says that Judas "went and hanged himself." So the
man thought he had better try again. This time his
finger came to rest on the admonition of Luke 10:37,
"Go, and do thou likewise." When he followed the same
procedure a third time, his finger fell on these words of
John 13:27, "What thou doest, do quickly."

But I would ye should understand, brethren, that
the things which happened unto me have fallen out
rather unto the furtherance of the gospel.
　　　　　　　　　　　　　　Philippians 1:12

Richard Storrs and Gordon Hall were students at
the same theological seminary. One Saturday toward
the end of the semester, Hall was preparing to go to
Braintree, Massachusetts, to preach, hoping that he
might receive the invitation to become the pastor. As
he was splitting some wood that afternoon, his hat fell
beneath the ax and was destroyed. He didn't have the
money to replace it and it was too cold to travel without
a hat, so he asked his friend to take his assignment.
Storrs preached and later accepted the call, and he remained the minister of that parish until his dying

day—a period of more than half a century! And although Hall had been disappointed with missing that opportunity, he sought other outlets for his talents and became a renowned foreign missionary.

For Further Study: Exodus 15:13; Exodus 33:12-15; 2 Samuel 22:29; Psalm 5:8; Isaiah 42:16; Isaiah 58:11.

God's Presence

Yea, though I walk through the valley of the shadow of death, I will fear no evil; for Thou art with me; Thy rod and Thy staff they comfort me.
Psalm 23:4

During World War II, Dr. Edward H. Friedman was on duty in an overseas army hospital. An American soldier by the name of Rothermel had just been brought in from the battlefield. His right leg was torn, his arms twisted, and part of his face was gone. He was in excruciating pain. As Friedman prepared for surgery, the young man said, "Don't worry, Doc, Jesus is with me!" His words kept ringing through the surgeon's mind as he worked over that mangled body. Later, as the exhausted doctor lay on his bed, he asked himself, "Is Rothermel's Jesus my Jesus?" Then he began reading the New Testament, and as a result he accepted Christ as his Savior. After the war, Friedman informed his parents that he had become a Christian. They had told him earlier that if he ever made that decision, as far as they were concerned he was dead. The words of that wounded soldier sustained the doctor as he walked the lonely pathway of rejection.

Have not I commanded thee? Be strong and of good courage; be not afraid, neither be thou dismayed; for the Lord thy God is with thee wherever thou goest.
Joshua 1:9

An ocean liner left a British port during World War II and headed for a harbor in the United States. Enemy subs and cruisers were scattered about, placing the ship in peril as it crossed the Atlantic. Therefore, the captain was given secret directions charting the route. Added were these instructions: "Keep straight on this course. Turn aside for nothing. If you need help, send a wireless message in code." After a few days out at sea, the crew spotted an enemy cruiser on the horizon. It appeared to be trailing them. The captain immediately sent a coded message: "Enemy cruiser sighted. What shall I do?" The reply came from an unseen vessel: "Keep straight on. I'm standing by." No friendly ship could be seen, but the captain kept the liner on course until it safely reached the port. Within a short time, a British warship glided quietly into the same harbor. Although it had been out of sight, it had protected the passenger vessel.

For Further Study: Genesis 16:13; Genesis 28:16; Psalm 139; Jeremiah 23:23,24; Jeremiah 32:18,19; Acts 17:24,27,28.

God's Will

And He said, Abba, Father, all things are possible unto Thee. Take away this cup from Me; nevertheless, not what I will, but what Thou wilt.
Mark 14:36

Years ago a minister was called to the home of a widow whose teenage daughter was the apple of her eye. She told the preacher that at the age of 3 the girl had been very ill, and the doctors said she would die. The mother admitted that she had accused God of cruelty and had prayed that He spare her daughter. She told Him she could never trust Him again if He did not do as she asked. God granted her request, in spite of what the doctors had said. For the next 13 years, she was her mother's pride and joy. But then she began to associate with bad companions. At the age of 17 she got into real trouble and broke her mother's heart. The tragic end of the story was told to the minister by that weeping woman when he arrived at her home that day. "My Janie is dead! She took her own life last night, and I found her in her room this morning." After several minutes of convulsive sobbing, she concluded, "O Pastor, how I wish God had taken her when she was 3 years old! How I wish I had yielded to God's will and not insisted on having my own way!"

> *For ye ought to say, If the Lord will, we shall live, and do this, or that.*　　　　　　　　　　*James 4:15*

When John Henry Jowett was a young man, he was so intent on pursuing a law career that he didn't consult the Lord about his vocation. One day he met a former Sunday school teacher, who asked him what he was going to do with his many talents. Jowett replied that he was studying to be a lawyer. Disappointed, his friend said, "I've prayed for years that you'd go into the ministry." This startled the brilliant young student and set him to thinking. Later Jowett wrote, "I then sought God's will in prayer and reverently obeyed His call. Now, after 35 years in His service, I can say that I've never regretted my choice."

For Further Study: Matthew 12:50; John 6:38-40; Romans 12:1,2; Hebrews 13:20,21; James 4:13-17.

Gospel

> *For to this end Christ both died, and rose, and revived, that He might be Lord both of the dead and living.*　　　　　　　　　　*Romans 14:9*

A young scholar approached the renowned English statesman Benjamin Disraeli. He had developed a new religion, and he had just written a book to explain its doctrines. The young man claimed that his newly devised creed surpassed in beauty the message of Christ and His sacrificial crucifixion on Calvary. Disraeli asked the young man about the success of the book's sales, only to hear him complain that he couldn't get anyone to buy it or to believe in his religion. The elderly statesman placed his hand on the young man's shoulder and said, "No, my boy, you will never get anyone to read your book and believe in your religion until you too have been crucified on a cross and risen from a tomb."

For Further Study: Mark 1:14,15; Romans 10:15-18; 1 Corinthians 9:16-18; 1 Corinthians 15:1-5; 2 Corinthians 4:3-6.

Heaven

And they shall see His face; and His name shall be in their foreheads. And there shall be no night there; and they need no lamp, neither light of the sun; for the Lord God giveth them light, and they shall reign forever and ever.　　　*Revelation 22:4,5*

A preacher once remarked to Fanny Crosby, "I think it is a great pity that the Master did not give you sight when He showered so many other gifts upon you." She replied quickly, "Do you know that if I had been able to make one petition at birth, it would have been that I should be born blind?" "Why?" asked the surprised clergyman. "Because when I get to heaven, the first face that shall ever gladden my sight will be that of my Savior!"

But I would not have you to be ignorant, brethren, concerning them who are asleep, that ye sorrow not, even as others who have no hope. For if we believe that Jesus died and rose again, even so them also who sleep in Jesus will God bring with Him.
1 Thessalonians 4:13,14

A missionary from the British Isles named Eric Barker spent more than 50 years in Portugal preaching the gospel, often under adverse conditions. During World War II, the situation became so critical that Barker was advised to send his wife and eight children to England for safety. His sister and her three children were also evacuated on the same ship. Although his beloved relatives were forced to leave, he remained behind to carry on the work. On the Lord's Day following their departure, he stood before his congregation and said, "I've just received word that all my family have arrived safely home!" He then proceeded with the service as usual. Later, the full meaning of his words became known to his people. Just before the meeting, he had learned that a submarine had torpedoed the ship and everyone on board had drowned. He knew that because all were believers they had reached a more "desired haven" (Psalm 107:30). Although Barker was overwhelmed with grief, he was able to rise above the circumstances by the grace of God and keep on working for the Lord. The knowledge that his family was enjoying the bliss of heaven comforted his heart.

For our light affliction, which is but for a moment, worketh for us a far more exceeding and eternal weight of glory.   *2 Corinthians 4:17*

The magazine *Wonderful Word* carried the story of an aged Christian Englishman. While he was laboring with another worker under the hot summer sun, he put down his heavy load to rest. As he sat by the road, an expensive limousine passed by. Its wealthy owner sat in the back seat, being chauffeured in luxurious ease. His fellow worker pointed to the passing auto and said, "Do you know the occupant of that car? He is an ungodly man, but he isn't having troubles like you. You believe that everything belongs to the Lord, you trust Him, and you serve Him; yet you still have to work hard in your old age for a meager living. How can you reconcile this with the love and justice of God?" With great earnestness the old man replied, "Are you testing me, sir? Couple heaven with it! Couple heaven with it!" This poor, elderly saint of God saw life's true source of

64

wealth, for he could look beyond his earthly condition to his eternal treasures.

And God shall wipe away all tears from their eyes; and there shall be no more death, neither sorrow, nor crying, neither shall there be any more pain; for the former things are passed away.
Revelation 21:4

Occasionally D. L. Moody told about a Christian woman who was always bright, cheerful, and optimistic, even though she was confined to her room because of illness. She lived in an attic apartment on the fifth floor of an old, rundown building. A friend decided to visit her one day and brought along another woman—a person of great wealth. Since there was no elevator, the two ladies began the long climb upward. When they reached the second floor, the well-to-do woman commented, "What a dark and filthy place!" Her friend replied, "It's better higher up." When they arrived at the third landing, the remark was made, "Things look even worse here." Again the reply, "It's better higher up." The two women finally reached the attic level, where they found the bedridden saint of God. A smile on her face radiated the joy that filled her heart. Although the room was clean and flowers were on the window sill, the wealthy visitor could not get over the stark surroundings in which this woman lived. She blurted out, "It must be very difficult for you to be here like this!" Without a moment's hesitation the shut-in responded, "It's better higher up." She was not looking at temporal things. With the eye of faith fixed on the eternal, she had found the secret of true satisfaction and contentment.

For our citizenship is in heaven, from which also we look for the Savior, the Lord Jesus Christ.
Philippians 3:20

The story is told of a nobleman who died very suddenly. Immediately his jester ran to tell the servants of the household that their master was dead. He said with gravity, "And where has he gone?" The servants replied, "Why to heaven, to be sure." "No," said the jester, "I am certain he has not gone to heaven." Somewhat surprised, the others asked him how he knew their master had not gone to heaven. The jester replied, "Because heaven is a long way off, and I've never known my master to take a long trip in his life but what he talked of it beforehand and made thorough preparations for it. I never heard him say a word about this journey, nor did I see him getting ready for it. Therefore, I am sure he has not gone to heaven!"

Looking unto Jesus, the author and finisher of our faith, who for the joy that was set before Him endured the cross, despising the shame, and is set down at the right hand of the throne of God.
                                                    Hebrews 12:2

Some years ago Arnold Olson, former president of the Evangelical Free Church of America, was speaking at a youth conference in northern Minnesota. He shared a room with an older minister who was deeply devoted to Christ. As the elderly man was shaving one morning, he paused and quite unexpectedly said, "Brother Olson, you won't be angry with me, will you, if I don't notice you when we get to heaven?" "Not at all," Olson assured him. "Well," he continued, "I figure I'll be so busy looking at Jesus for the first thousand years that I'll have little time for you." That servant of God held one person, the Lord Jesus, uppermost in his mind—even while he was shaving!

For Further Study: Philippians 1:21-23; 1 Thessalonians 4:16,17; Hebrews 11:16; Revelation 21.

Hell

And whosoever was not found written in the book of life was cast into the lake of fire.   *Revelation 20:15*

An old Scottish preacher had to go past a glass factory each day on his way to the church. On one occasion he had a little extra time, and since the factory door was open, he decided to look inside. There before him was a large, blazing furnace. The minister gazed into the white, blue, and purple mass of liquid flame, and the intense heat almost seared his face. As he turned to leave, a workman standing in the shadows nearby overheard him exclaim, "Ho, mon! What shall hell be like!" Several days later, the man came to the pastor at the church. "You don't know me," he said, "but the other day when you stepped into the furnace room I heard what you said. Now every time I open that hot door to stoke the fire, the words ring in my mind, 'What shall hell be like!' I have come to you, sir, to find out how to be saved. I don't ever want to know the reality of that place."

Keep yourselves in the love of God, looking for the mercy of our Lord Jesus Christ unto eternal life. And of some have compassion, making a difference; and others save with fear, pulling them out of the fire, hating even the garment spotted by the flesh.   *Jude 21-23*

A church was looking for a pastor, so they invited several candidates to come and preach for them. One minister spoke on the text, "The wicked shall be turned into hell." The head elder was not in favor of him. A few weeks later, another preacher came and used the same Scripture for his sermon. This time the head elder said, "He's good! Let's call him." The other board members were surprised, and one of them asked, "Why did you like him? He used the same text as the other minister." "True," replied the chairman, "but when the second man emphasized that the lost will be turned into hell, he said it with tears in his eyes and with concern in his voice. The first preacher almost seemed to gloat over it."

For Further Study: Matthew 5:28-30; Luke 12:1-5; Luke 16:19-31; John 5:28,29.

Home/Family

The following story was told by a father who
learned how unwise it was to neglect spending time
with his son: "One year ago today I sat at my desk with
a month's bills and overdue accounts before me when
my bright-faced young boy rushed in and impetuously
announced, 'Happy birthday, Dad! Mom says you're 55
today, so I'm going to give you 55 kisses, one for each
year.' He began to make good on his word when I
exclaimed, 'Oh, Andy, not now; I'm too busy!' He
became silent, and when I looked up I saw that his big
blue eyes were filled with tears. Apologetically I said,
'You can finish tomorrow.' He made no reply, but he
was unable to conceal his disappointment as he quietly
walked away. That same evening I called to him, 'Come
and finish those kisses now, Andy.' Either he didn't
hear me or he wasn't in the mood, for there was no
response. Two months later, as a result of an accident,
God took him home to heaven. His body was laid to rest
in a little cemetery near a place where he loved to play.
The robin's note was never sweeter than my son's voice,
and the turtledove that cooed to its nestlings was never
so gentle as the little one who left unfinished his love-
imposed task. If only I could tell him how much I regret
those thoughtless words I spoke, and how my heart is
aching now because of my unkind actions. Instead, I sit
here thinking, 'Why didn't I return his love? Why did I
grieve his young heart that was so full of tenderness
and affection?'"

which dwelt first in thy grandmother, Lois, and thy
mother, Eunice; and I am persuaded that in thee
also.   *2 Timothy 1:3-5*

Godly parents leave an unforgettable impression on their families. This is often evidenced by the love and respect they receive from their children. Take, for example, the thoughtfulness that William McKinley showed to his mother. As lawyer, congressman, Governor of Ohio, and as President of the United States, he kept in touch with her every day. When he didn't see her, he wrote or telegraphed. In mid-October of 1897, he quietly left the White House and took a train to Canton just so he could walk to church with her again. When she became ill, he arranged to have a special train standing by at full steam, ready to take him to her bedside. Then one night she did call for him. Immediately he wired, "Tell Mother I'll be there." Mrs. McKinley died December 12, 1897, in the arms of her 54-year-old son. Her gentle, Christian virtues helped mold the President's character, for when he was gunned down in Buffalo, New York, about 4 years later, he showed no bitterness toward his assassin. With Christian courage he said, "God's will be done." Before he died, he asked to hear once again the hymn, "Nearer, My God, to Thee," which his mother had taught him.

And if it seem evil unto you to serve the Lord, choose
you this day whom ye will serve, whether the gods
which your fathers served that were on the other
side of the river, or the gods of the Amorites, in
whose land ye dwell; but as for me and my house,
we will serve the Lord.   *Joshua 24:15*

A Christian periodical told the story of a farmer who hung a beautiful plaque in his home. It bore this well-known motto: BUT AS FOR ME AND MY HOUSE, WE WILL SERVE THE LORD. It expressed his deepest feelings, for he prayed daily that his entire family might serve the Lord. The last clause applied to everyone except his oldest son, who persistently refused to accept Christ—much to his parents' sorrow. One day the father was alone with him in the room where the motto hung, and his eyes filled with tears as he said with deep emotion, "Henry, my dear boy, I just cannot be a liar any longer. You belong to my house, but you don't want to serve the Lord. I'm going to hang another sign right beneath this plaque with the words, 'Except Henry.' It hurts me to do it, but I must be true to the Lord." The father's sincere words so impressed the young man that he began thinking seriously about his need of becoming a Christian. The Holy Spirit convicted him of his sinfulness, and before his dad was able to put up the second sign he gave his heart to the Lord. What rejoicing came to that home! Now the father could truthfully say that he and his entire house were one in the Lord.

Hear my prayer, O Lord, give ear to my supplications; in Thy faithfulness answer me, and in Thy righteousness.　　　　*Psalm 143:1*

Some years ago a minister in Cincinnati concluded his sermon with this evangelistic appeal: "If there's someone here who desires help in getting to know the Lord, will you please raise your hand?" A young fellow quickly stood up and said with emotion, "Please pray for me, sir. The burden of my sin is too heavy to bear." After the service, the minister counseled with the man until he found peace by trusting the Savior. For 8 years he had wandered around the country without contacting his parents. The pastor advised him to write to them immediately. That very day he penned a letter describing his conversion and how it all came about. He also asked their forgiveness for his past disobedience. Later a reply came from his mother. His eyes filled with tears as he read, "My dear son, the joy of receiving your letter was mixed with sadness. As near as I can tell, you must have accepted Jesus Christ at the same hour your father went home to heaven. He had been sick for a long time, and that day he was very restless.

He tossed from side to side on his bed, crying out in misery, 'O dear Lord, please save my poor, wandering boy.' Just as he slipped away, he began to murmur the same sentence again, but death sealed his lips before he could finish his plea. He was still praying when he went into the presence of Jesus. Son, I'm sure that one of the reasons you became a Christian was Dad's unceasing intercession."

A foolish son is a grief to his father, and bitterness to her that bore him.   Proverbs 17:25

In *Moody Monthly,* P. W. Philpott related a touching story about a fine British Christian. The man was successful in business, and his well-educated son was as highly respected and honored as his father. But one day to everyone's surprise the young man was charged with embezzlement. At his trial he appeared nonchalant and arrogant about his sinful actions. When the judge told him to stand up for sentencing, he still seemed unrepentant. Then, hearing a slight scuffle on the other side of the room, he turned to see that his aged father had also risen. The once-erect head and straight shoulders were now bowed low with shame. He had stood to be identified with his boy and to receive the verdict as though it were being pronounced upon himself. Suddenly his son realized the terrible grief he was inflicting on him, and tears welled up in his eyes. He had tarnished the family name by his behavior. Now his poor father was caught in the backwash of his son's evil deed, although he had done everything he could to keep him on the straight and narrow path.

And these words, which I command thee this day, shall be in thine heart; and thou shalt teach them diligently unto thy children, and shalt talk of them when thou sittest in thine house, and when thou walkest by the way, and when thou liest down, and when thou risest up.   Deuteronomy 6:6,7

Among the more than 3,000 Americans who have received the Congressional Medal of Honor is a father-son combination. The father won it for a single act of bravery in a crucial battle of the Civil War. By the time he retired in 1909, he was the ranking officer in the United States Army and one of the most famous soldiers of his era. But his son rose to even greater fame. In 1941 he headed up the U.S. forces in the Philippines, and he led the gallant defense of the Bataan peninsula and the island of Corregidor. Although the battles fought there ended in defeat, the bravery displayed by the Americans and their leader provided inspiration to thousands of soldiers and sailors, as well as to millions of workers on the homefront. This man's name was General Douglas MacArthur, and his father was Arthur MacArthur, Jr. No doubt the son's greatness can be traced in part to the outstanding heritage left to him by his dad.

> *And he did that which was right in the sight of the Lord, and walked in the ways of David, his father, and declined neither to the right hand, nor to the left.*	*2 Chronicles 34:2*

Several years ago the *Christian Life and Faith* magazine presented some unusual facts about two families. In 1677 an immoral man married a licentious woman. Nineteen hundred descendants came from the generations begun by that union. Of these, 771 were criminals, 250 were arrested for various offenses, 60 were thieves, and 39 were convicted of murder. Forty of the women were known to have venereal disease. These people spent a combined total of 1300 years behind bars and cost the state of New York nearly $3 million.

The other family was the Edwards family. The third generation included Jonathan Edwards, who was the great New England revival preacher and who became president of Princeton University. Of the 1,344 descendants, many were college presidents and professors. One hundred eighty-six became ministers of the gospel, and many others were active in their churches. Eighty-six were state senators, three were

Congressmen, thirty were judges, and one became Vice President of the United States. No reference was made of anyone spending time in jail or in the poorhouse.

The rod and reproof give wisdom, but a child left to himself bringeth his mother to shame.
Proverbs 29:15

A brokenhearted mother asked a minister to visit her son who was in prison. She handed him a photograph and a letter and said, "Will you show him my picture? He never answers my letters; maybe this will touch his heart." The man called at the prison, and the young man was brought in under guard. When he was presented with the photograph, he said without emotion, "Yes, that's my mother. Her hair is more gray, but that's her." And then handing the photograph back along with the letter (which he refused to read), he said in a voice full of bitterness, "When you see her again, return these. I don't want them. It was in my mother's home I played the first game of cards, and she gave me my first drink. Those two things, drinking and gambling, have put me here for 15 years. And now she sends me her picture with belated love. Take them back and tell her that I hate both her and the religion she professes!"

Lo, children are an heritage from the Lord.
Psalm 127:3

A preacher tells of being entertained by a couple who had two teenage boys. He said that when he entered the house he immediately sensed that it was a warm and loving home. During the course of his stay, he noticed that the carpet in the living room was tattered and torn, and he wondered about it. Before he left, the mother related a story that accounted for its condition. She said that one day several boys from the neighborhood were having a good time in the living room. She preferred that they play elsewhere, so she asked them to leave. "But where will we go?" they asked. "How about your place?" she suggested, nodding to one of them. "Not a chance," replied the boy. "We're not allowed to invite kids in." Then she said to another, "How about your house?" He too answered quickly, "Oh, Mom wouldn't let us mess up her living room!" The mother quickly sensed that her home was the only one where the boys felt free to come and have fun. From then on, they were always welcome. "After I heard her story," said the preacher, "that tattered rug seemed almost beautiful—it was worn out in helping make those boys good."

But if any provide not for his own, and specially for those of his own house, he hath denied the faith, and is worse than an infidel.   1 Timothy 5:8

A New Zealand publication called *The Reaper* contained some interesting advice to moms and dads written by teenagers in jail. Here in essence is what these young lawbreakers said: (1) Keep cool; don't lose your temper in the crunch. Kids need the reassurance that comes from controlled responses. (2) Don't get strung out on booze or pills. We lose respect for parents who tell us to behave one way while they are behaving the other. (3) Bug us a little; be strict and consistent in giving out discipline. (4) Don't blow your class; keep the dignity of parenthood. (5) Light a candle; show us the way. (6) Be strong. Don't be afraid of us. If you catch us lying, stealing, or being cruel, get tough. When we need punishment, dish it out. But then let us know that you still love us. (7) Call our bluff; make it clear that you mean what you say. If you collapse, we will know we beat you down, and we will not be happy about the "victory." (8) Be honest with us. Tell the truth no matter what. Be straight about it.

For Further Study: Genesis 25:27-34; Genesis 26:34,35; Genesis 37:3; 1 Samuel 2:12-17, 22-26; 1 Samuel 3:11-14; Proverbs 22:6; Ephesians 6:1-4.

Honesty

Diverse weights, and diverse measures, both of them are alike an abomination to the Lord. Even a child is known by his doings, whether his work be pure, and whether it be right.　　　*Proverbs 20:10,11*

A boy went to a lady's house to sell some berries he had picked. "Yes, I'll buy some," said the lady as she took the pail and went inside. Without concern for the berries, the boy stayed at the door, whistling to some birds perched in a cage. "Don't you want to come in and see that I don't take more than I should? How do you know I won't cheat you?" she asked. The boy responded from the porch, "I'm not worried. Besides, you'd get the worst of it." "Get the worst of it," said the lady. "What do you mean by that?" "Oh, I would only lose a few berries, but you would make yourself a thief."

Better is the poor that walketh in his uprightness, than he that is perverse in his ways, though he be rich.　　　*Proverbs 28:6*

A sensitive, hard-working man named Sa'ad lives in the city of Zarayed, one of Cairo's garbage dumps. He works long hours collecting trash so that he can eke out a livelihood for his wife and children. Often his profit is little more than 50 cents a day. Sa'ad is one of thousands who are trapped in a hopeless prison of poverty. One day he found a gold watch valued at nearly $2,000, but he returned it to its owner. Why? Sa'ad is a Christian, and he believes it's wrong to keep what doesn't belong to him.

He that is faithful in that which is least is faithful also in much; and he that is unjust in the least is unjust also in much.　　　*Luke 16:10*

A bank employee was due for a good promotion. One day at lunch the president of the bank, who happened to be standing behind the clerk in the cafeteria, saw him slip two pats of butter under his slice of bread so they wouldn't be seen by the cashier. That little act of dishonesty cost him his promotion. Just 10 cents' worth of butter made the difference. The bank president reasoned that if an employee cannot be trusted in little things, he cannot be trusted at all.

A righteous man hateth lying, but a wicked man is loathsome, and cometh to shame.　　　*Proverbs 13:5*

The story is told of four high school boys who could not resist the temptation to skip classes. Each had been smitten with a bad case of spring fever. The next morning they showed up at school and reported to the teacher that their car had had a flat tire. Much to their relief, she smiled and said, "Well, you missed a quiz yesterday, so take your seats and get out a pencil and paper." Still smiling, she waited as they settled down and got ready for her questions. Then she said, "First question—which tire was flat?"

Thou shalt not raise a false report: put not thine hand with the wicked to be an unrighteous witness.　　　*Exodus 23:1*

A 12-year-old boy was the important witness in a lawsuit. One of the lawyers, after questioning him severely, asked, "Your father has been telling you how to testify, hasn't he?" "Yes," said the boy. "Now," pursued the lawyer, "just tell us how your father told you to testify." "Well," replied the boy modestly, "Father told me the lawyers might try to tangle me in my testimony; but if I would just be careful to tell the truth, I would say the same thing every time."

Thou shalt destroy those who speak falsehood; the
Lord will abhor the bloody and deceitful man.
Psalm 5:6

In the book *Eternity Shut in a Span* is the story of a night watchman who was a defendant in court. He had been on duty at a railway crossing on the night of an accident. A train had struck a car, resulting in serious injury to the occupants. No one else had seen the crash. The watchman testified that he had swung his lantern to warn the driver. The court found him blameless and placed the responsibility for the accident on the motorist. The watchman's friends immediately began to praise him for his faithfulness in waving the lamp. Greatly relieved by the verdict, he whispered, "And all the time I was afraid they would ask me if the lantern was lit."

And, indeed, ye do it toward all the brethren who
are in all Macedonia. But we beseech you, brethren,
that ye increase more and more, and that ye study
to be quiet, and to do your own business, and to
work with your own hands, as we commanded you,
that ye may walk honestly toward them that are
outside, and that ye may have lack of nothing.
1 Thessalonians 4:10-12

When Henry Bosch was a boy, he worked with his father during the summer months. Each morning they would stop to pick up the early edition of a local newspaper to read at coffeebreak. One time when they arrived at work, Mr. Bosch discovered he had taken two of that day's papers by mistake. He thought first of paying the man the extra dime the following morning, but then he said, "No, I'd better take it back right now. Someone might miss getting the morning news. And I don't want the owner, who isn't a Christian, to think I'm dishonest." So he got into his car and drove several miles to return the paper.

About a week later, some expensive items were shoplifted from that same general store. When the officers and the owner calculated the time of day they must have been taken, the proprietor said that only two people had been there during that period—Henry's father (who always stopped for a paper) and one other man. The storekeeper immediately eliminated Mr. Bosch as a suspect, saying to the officers, "I know John is honest. Just last week he came all the way back here to return a newspaper he'd taken by mistake. The other man must be the thief." The police apprehended the culprit, who made a full confession. John Bosch's honesty and Christian character had borne fruit.

To do righteousness and justice is more acceptable to the Lord than sacrifice.   Proverbs 21:3

A band of peasants was breaking into a mill to take some corn. "What do you think you're doing?" Martin Luther asked. Terrified, one of the men answered, "We know it's wrong to steal, but after all, we have to live." With indignation the church leader responded, "I do not know that one must live. But I do know that one must be honest."

For Further Study: Deuteronomy 25:13-16; Proverbs 12:22; Isaiah 33:15,16; 2 Corinthians 4:1,2; Colossians 3:22; 1 Peter 2:11,12.

Humility/Pride

Blessed are the meek; for they shall inherit the earth.   Matthew 5:5

The following story comes from the *Choice Gleanings Calendar:* "A little western college needed money. The buildings were shabby, the salaries underpaid. A stranger appeared on the campus and asked a man who was washing a wall where he could find the president. 'I think you can see him at his house at twelve,' was the reply. The visitor went as directed and met the president, whom he recognized, although in different clothes, as the man he had found scrubbing. The next day a letter came with a gift of $50,000 for the college. The spirit of service on the part of the president had appealed effectively to him." Because the benefactor saw a man who was not too proud to help where needed, even though it involved what some might term a menial task, he was moved to contribute generously to the school.

Let another man praise thee, and not thine own mouth; a stranger, and not thine own lips.
Proverbs 27:2

When everything is going well or if people praise us highly, pride may fill our hearts and spill over as boastful speech. This happened to a young man shortly after he had received an award for outstanding achievement. He took too seriously the extravagant praise of the one who made the presentation. When he got home, he repeated to his mother all that had been said. Then he paused and asked, "How many great men do you suppose there are in the world today?" Her wise reply was, "One less than you think, my son."

A man's pride shall bring him low, but honor shall uphold the humble in spirit.   *Proverbs 29:23*

George Bernard Shaw once boasted about his great skill at making a good cup of coffee. A country parson heard about it and wrote to ask him how he did it. Shaw responded by giving the secret, but added, "I hope this is a genuine request and not just a trick to secure my autograph." The preacher could not let the implication of that remark go unanswered. So he sent him a letter in reply. It read, "Accept my thanks for the directions to make coffee. I wrote in good faith. To convince you of that, however, allow me to return what it is obvious you infinitely prize, but which is of no value to me—your autograph."

But he that is greatest among you shall be your
servant.   *Matthew 23:11*

One day when George Washington was replacing some stones that a member of his riding party had knocked off a rock fence, someone remarked, "General, you are too big a man to be doing that." Looking at what he had done, Washington replied, "Oh, no, I'm just the right size."

c.c. Sept 15
1985 *And whosoever shall exalt himself shall be abased; and he that shall humble himself shall be exalted.*
                     Matthew 23:12

A truly humble man is hard to find, yet God often chooses to honor selfless people. Shortly after Booker T. Washington, the renowned black educator, took over the presidency of Tuskegee Institute in Alabama, he was walking through an exclusive section of town when he was stopped by a wealthy white woman. Not knowing the famous Mr. Washington by sight, she asked if he would like to earn a few dollars by chopping wood for her. Because he had no pressing business at the moment, Professor Washington smiled, rolled up his sleeves, and proceeded to do the humble chore she had requested. When he was finished, he carried the logs into the house and stacked them by the fireplace. A little girl recognized him and later revealed his identity to the lady. The next morning the embarrassed woman went to see Mr. Washington in his office at the Institute and apologized profusely. "It's perfectly all right, Madam," he replied. "Occasionally I enjoy a little manual labor. Besides, it's always a delight to do something for a friend."

Let us not be desirous of vainglory, provoking one
another, envying one another.   *Galatians 5:26*

cc. Sept 15
1985 For many years Sir Walter Scott was the leading literary figure in the British Empire. No one could write

80

as well as he. Then the works of Lord Byron began to appear, and their greatness was immediately evident. Soon an anonymous critic praised his poems in a London paper. He declared that in the presence of these brilliant works of poetic genius, Scott could no longer be considered the leading poet of England. It was later discovered that the unnamed reviewer had been none other than Sir Walter Scott himself!

> *When pride cometh, then cometh shame; but with the lowly is wisdom.*   *Proverbs 11:2*

The following interesting story is attributed to Martin Luther: Two mountain goats meet on a narrow ledge just wide enough for one of the animals. On the left is a sheer cliff, and on the right a deep lake. The two face each other. What should they do? They can't back up—that would be too dangerous; they can't turn around, because the ledge is too narrow. Now if the goats had no more sense than some people, they would meet head-on and start butting each other till they fall into the lake below. Luther said that goats have better sense than this. One lies down on the trail and lets the other literally walk over him—and both are safe. One of them must be willing to lie down and let the other pass over him. If they were like some people, they would argue about who should lie down and who should walk over; but evidently "goat-sense" is common sense!

> *Let no man deceive himself. If any man among you seemeth to be wise in this age, let him become a fool, that he may be wise.*   *1 Corinthians 3:18*

An officer who had just been promoted to the rank of colonel was sitting at his desk glancing proudly at the "birds" on his shoulders. A private walked in through the open door of his new office, saluted, and was about to speak when the colonel said, "Just a minute, soldier. I have to make an important telephone call." He dialed a number and said, "Hello, General Cool. I'm returning your call. You would like to have me meet with you and three other generals? Today at 1400 hours? Yes, I can be there." Putting down the receiver and with a smug expression on his face, he turned to the soldier, "Now, private, what can I do for you?" "I've been sent to hook up your telephone, sir!" came the reply.

For Further Study: Genesis 41:16; Psalm 9:2; Proverbs 25:6,7; Matthew 18:2-4; Luke 22:24-27; 2 Corinthians 12:5-12.

Hypocrisy

Knowest thou not this of old, since man was placed upon earth, that the triumphing of the wicked is short, and the joy of the hypocrite but for a moment?   *Job 20:4,5*

A pastor told an amusing but pointed story about an unsaved man who was on his way to attend a costume ball one Sunday evening. He was wearing a red suit with a tail and a skintight mask with horns. He looked like Satan; that is, he conformed to the false but widely accepted picture of the devil. As he hurried along, he was caught in a sudden rainstorm, so he sought shelter in a church where the service was just ending. When he ran into the building, he shocked the members, who thought he was the real thing. A flash of lightning and a clap of thunder added to the illusion. The congregation panicked and rushed for the rear exits. The intruder thought the church had been struck and was on fire, so he raced after them. Everyone got out except one elderly lady. Turning in fear, she stretched out her hands and pleaded for mercy, "Oh, devil, please don't hurt me. I know I've been a member of this church for 30 years, but I've really been on your side all the time!"

For Further Study: Job 8:13-15; Psalm 101:7; Hosea 10:1-4; Matthew 21:28-32; Matthew 23:1-33; Luke 20:45-47.

Influence

For none of us liveth to himself, and no man dieth to himself.   *Romans 14:7*

One time the electrical workers in Paris called a general strike. Soon after the walkout began, a child of one of the laborers became seriously ill. When the physician arrived, he told the mother that the little girl would need immediate surgery to save her life. There was no time to take her to the hospital, so the doctor quickly prepared the kitchen table for an emergency operation. Darkness was falling as the final sanitary precautions were completed. The doctor flipped on the light switch—but there was no electricity. It was impossible to perform the surgery. Just then the father burst into the room and exclaimed, "Hurrah! The strike is complete. There isn't a light burning in Paris!"

The fruit of the righteous is a tree of life; and he that winneth souls is wise.   *Proverbs 11:30*

Years ago, an article was published that cited a number of men whose faithful witness through books and pamphlets had brought many people to the Lord. Richard Gibbs, an elderly Puritan doctor, wrote *The Bruised Reed.* A copy came into the hands of Richard Baxter and resulted in his conversion. Baxter later authored a volume entitled *Saints' Rest and Call to the Unconverted.* By it many sinners were led to Jesus, including Philip Doddridge, who became a famous preacher, hymnwriter, and the president of a theological seminary. Doddridge wrote the well-circulated book *The Rise and Progress of Religion in the Soul,* which proved a rich blessing to countless numbers. William Wilberforce read it, was convicted of sin, and became a Christian statesman. After being instrumental in freeing slaves, he penned *Practical View of Christianity.* This changed the life of Leigh Richmond, who in turn became a world-famous writer of tracts that influenced thousands to seek the Lord. Yes, the "fruit of the righteous" is a "family tree" of converts who keep branching out to others.

Be not deceived: Evil company corrupts good morals.   *1 Corinthians 15:33*

A farmer was bothered by some crows that were pulling up his young corn. So he loaded his shotgun and crawled unseen along a fence row, determined to get a shot at the marauders. Now, the farmer had a very "sociable" parrot who made friends with everybody. Seeing the noisy offenders in the field, the bird flew over and joined them (just being sociable, of course). His owner saw the crows but didn't notice the family pet. He took careful aim, and—BANG! When he climbed over the fence to pick up the crows he had shot, he found his parrot—badly ruffled and with a broken wing, but still alive. He tenderly carried it home, where his children met him. They saw that their pet was injured, and they tearfully asked, "What happened to Polly, Father?" Before he could answer, the parrot spoke up. "Bad company! Bad company!"

Ye are the light of the world. A city that is set on an hill cannot be hidden. Neither do men light a lamp, and put it under a bushel, but on a lampstand, and it giveth light unto all that are in the house.
Matthew 5:14,15

The story was told by Harry Rimmer of a fine young man who entered the army. As a lad he had formed the habit of studying his Bible in his bedroom each evening and then kneeling down to pray. He faced a real test the first night in the barracks, for he was surrounded by scores of rough servicemen preparing to retire. Many of them were joking and cursing loudly, so he considered lying down on his bunk, concealing his Bible under the blanket, and reading it, hoping that no one would notice. But then he told himself, "I'm a

Christian! I must take my stand for the Lord. I won't hide my faith. I'll do just as I did at home!" The courageous young man took his Bible and, after quietly reading a chapter, knelt and offered a silent prayer. When the men noticed his actions, a few sneered, but in about 2 minutes the barracks became quiet as some who respected the new recruit hushed the others. He felt like a goldfish in a glass bowl. After a while the talk began again, but the cursing stopped. The next night when he opened his Bible, eight of the other men dug out their Bibles and did the same. Within a month everyone in the outfit respected the young Christian so much that they would defend him against anyone who would criticize him. Rimmer said, "They brought their troubles and questions to him to be settled, and he influenced more men for Christ than half a dozen chaplains could have in a year of Sundays."

Wherefore, as by one man sin entered into the world, and death by sin, and so death passed upon all men, for all have sinned. Romans 5:12

A man was trying to convince an acquaintance that one individual can make a lasting impression on others. After a rather heated discussion, his friend continued to doubt this principle. To prove his point, the first man declared that he would introduce a new word into the English language. That night he chalked on walls and pavements throughout Dublin, Ireland, the four letters Q-U-I-Z, which he had chosen at random from the alphabet. The next morning everyone who saw this unusual expression was baffled by it. One person after another would ask, "What does it mean?" It wasn't long until the newspapers took up the query, and eventually this strange-sounding syllable was on the lips of everyone. Thus the term "quiz" was incorporated into the language as a synonym for "questioning." The originator had won his argument. He had left a lasting impression on many people by creating one new English word.

Howbeit, Jesus permitted him not, but saith unto him, Go home to thy friends, and tell them what great things the Lord hath done for thee, and hath had compassion on thee.   *Mark 5:19*

The great British preacher Alexander Maclaren of the 19th century was delighted one Lord's Day to see a well-known skeptic in his congregation. After the service he told the man that for the next 4 weeks he would be speaking on the main doctrines of the Christian faith. The nonbeliever came to every service and listened attentively. On the fourth Sunday the visitor declared that he had accepted Christ. When Maclaren asked which message had brought him to this decision, he replied, "Your sermons, sir, were helpful, but they were not what finally persuaded me to become a Christian. A few weeks ago as I was leaving church I noticed an elderly lady with a radiant face. Because she was making her way with difficulty along the icy street, I offered to help her. As we walked along together, she looked up at me and said, 'I wonder if you know my Savior, Jesus Christ? He is everything in the world to me. I want you to love Him too.' Those few words touched my heart, and when I got home, I knelt down and received the Savior. Right then I resolved to be His disciple and to unite with His church!"

By this perceive we the love of God, because He laid down His life for us; and we ought to lay down our lives for the brethren.   *1 John 3:16*

Never underestimate the tremendous influence you can wield through patient suffering for Jesus' sake. An incident in a French juvenile reformatory illustrates this truth. When a particularly rebellious boy stabbed another youth, inflicting a minor wound, he was sentenced to 3 months in a dark cell on a bread-and-water diet. He was afraid of the dark, and the prospect of what lay ahead terrified him. The wounded boy, who was a Christian, volunteered to take his place. The director accepted this suggestion on the condition that the guilty lad bring the bread and water to the other boy each day. On the sixth day he broke down and asked to take the punishment himself. The suffering of that Christian lad had touched his heart, and soon the guilty boy became a believer in Christ.

For Further Study: 1 Kings 22:42,43; 2 Chronicles 29-31; Luke 11:33; Philippians 2:12-16; 1 Peter 2:11,12; 1 Peter 3:13-16.

Kindness

And beside this, giving all diligence, add to your faith virtue; and to virtue, knowledge; and to knowledge, self-control; and to self-control, patience; and to patience, godliness; and to godliness, brotherly kindness; and to brotherly kindness, love.
2 Peter 1:5-7

A smalltown mayor was known for his godliness and his genuine interest in others. One day he warmly greeted a young man who had just returned to the community from prison. Six months afterward, the youth stopped him on the street and said, "Sir, I want to thank you for what you did for me." "What do you mean?" asked the mayor. "When I came home from prison, you spoke to me in a way that made me realize you really cared for me. Your concern turned me around, and I have accepted Christ as my Savior." Little did that mayor realize at the time what an impact his kind words would have upon that young man!

Look not every man on his own things, but every man also on the things of others.
Philippians 2:4

Many years ago the *Christian Herald* carried this story: "On a cold Sunday morning in February, a gentleman was hastily walking through the snow.

Suddenly he noticed a bright-looking little boy standing on the sidewalk with his cap in his hand and his eyes fixed on one spot on the pavement. As he approached, the lad looked up at him, pointed to the place, and said, 'Please don't step there, sir. That's where I slipped and fell down.' What a different world this would be if all Christians were as thoughtful as that boy in warning others against dangers, whether temporal or spiritual."

> *Blessed is he that considereth the poor; the Lord will deliver him in time of trouble.*
>
> *Psalm 41:1*

At one end of a truck terminal in the Midwest is a fuel supply company with a high fence around it. Nearby is a railroad, and each day several freight trains pass by. A worker noticed that the owner of the yard, a Christian, often threw chunks of coal over the fence at various places along the track. One day he asked the man why he did this. With some embarrassment he replied, "A poor elderly woman lives across the street, and I know that her old-age pension is inadequate to buy enough coal. After the trains go by, she walks along and picks up the pieces she thinks have fallen from the coal car behind the engine. Her eyesight is failing, and she doesn't realize that diesels have replaced steam locomotives. I don't want to disappoint her, so I throw some pieces over the fence to help her." That is Christianity in action!

> *A man hath joy by the answer of his mouth; and a word spoken in due season, how good is it!*
>
> *Proverbs 15:23*

Writing in the *Sunshine Magazine*, Maxine Dowd Jensen related this personal experience: "The second year I was married, my husband opened an envelope and then looked over at me. His brow was furrowed and his mouth a little awry as he said, 'Maxine, this is April. My birthday's in July.' 'I know,' I replied, 'but I saw this card. The sentiment is so appropriate. The card wouldn't be there if I waited till July. And if I bought it and brought it home, I'd put it away and forget I had it. So I just thought I'd send it now.' "

Bless them who persecute you; bless, and curse not.   *Romans 12:14*

A soldier heard General Robert E. Lee speak to the President in complimentary terms about an officer and was greatly astonished. "General," he said, "do you know that this man you speak of so highly is one of your worst enemies and misses no opportunity to malign you?" "Yes," said the general, "but the President asked for my opinion of him. He did not ask for his opinion of me."

And if ye do good to them who do good to you, what thanks have ye? For sinners also do even the same.   *Luke 6:33*

The following experience was related by R. L. Sharpe: "When I was just a lad, my father called me to go with him to old Mr. Trussel's blacksmith shop. He had left a rake and a hoe to be repaired, and when we got there they were fixed like new. Father handed him some money for the work, but Mr. Trussel refused to take it. 'No,' he said, 'there's no charge for that little job.' My father kept insisting, but I shall never forget that great man's reply. 'Ed,' he said, 'can't you let a Christian do something now and then—*just to stretch his soul?*' That short but effective sermon set me to thinking. I since have found the great joy and quiet happiness that come from doing little things for Jesus, and in the process I'm 'stretching my soul.' "

*Pure religion and undefiled before God and the
Father is this: to visit the fatherless and widows in
their affliction.*   *James 1:27*

This story about President Lincoln appeared in the
Gospel Herald years ago. Many people were waiting to
see him one day in 1864, and among them was a
delicate-looking boy of about 15. The President, noticing that he was pale and faint, disregarded some dignitaries who were first in line. Lincoln said to the boy,
"Come here, son, and tell me what you want." Advanc-
ing slowly and timidly, the young man said in a weak
voice, "Mr. President, I was a drummer in a regiment,
but I became sick and have been in the hospital for
many weeks. This is the first time I've been able to get
out, and I was hoping you could do something for me."
Lincoln looked at him kindly and asked him where he
lived. "I have no home," he answered. "Where is your
father?" "He died in the army." "Where is your
mother?" continued the President. "My mother is dead
also. I have no brothers, sisters, or friends." Beginning
to sob, the teenager concluded, "Nobody cares for me!"
Lincoln's eyes filled with tears. He took a pencil and
wrote a note to an official, who would act upon his request immediately. The note said, "Care for this poor
boy." The distressed lad never forgot that act of
compassion.

For Further Study: Deuteronomy 22:1; Zechariah 7:9,10;
John 19:25-27; Galatians 6:1,2; Colossians 3:12-14.

Little Things

*Dead flies cause the ointment of the perfumer to
send forth an evil odor; so doth a little folly him
that is in reputation for wisdom and honor.*
                              Ecclesiastes 10:1

When William McKinley was President of the
United States, he had to make a decision about the ap-

pointment of an ambassador to a foreign country. The two candidates were equally qualified, so McKinley searched his mind for some "yardstick" by which he might measure the true character of the men. Later he revealed that the unkindness of one of them was the determining factor in his decision. Many years earlier, when McKinley was still a Congressman, he had observed an inconsiderate act by one of the men. He recalled boarding a streetcar at the rush hour and getting the last vacant seat. Soon an elderly woman got on, carrying a heavy clothesbasket. No one offered her a seat, so she walked the length of the car and stood in the aisle, hardly able to keep her balance as the vehicle swayed from side to side. One of the men McKinley was later to consider for ambassador was sitting next to where she was standing. Instead of helping her, he deliberately shifted his newspaper so it would look like he hadn't seen her. When McKinley saw this, he walked down the aisle, took her basket, and offered her his seat. The man was unaware that anyone was watching, but his little act of selfishness later deprived him of what may have been the crowning honor of his lifetime.

For Further Study: Proverbs 6:10,11; Song of Solomon 2:15; 1 Corinthians 5:1-6.

Love

Greater love hath no man than this, that a man lay down his life for his friends.   *John 15:13*

In a hospital in a small midwestern town lay an infant girl who had been critically injured. She had lost a great amount of blood and urgently needed a transfusion. But no one could be found who had her rare blood type. Finally it was discovered that her 7-year-old brother had the same type of blood. The doctor took him into his office, held the youngster on his knee, and said, "Son, your sister is very, very sick. Unless we can help her, I'm afraid the angels are going to take her to heaven. Are you willing to give blood to your baby sister?" The young boy's face turned pale, and his eyes widened with fright and uncertainty. He appeared to be in great mental agony, but after a minute or so he half-whispered, "Yes, I will." The physician smiled reassuringly and said, "That's a fine boy; I knew you would." The transfusion took place, but the 7-year-old, watching the tube carrying the life-giving fluid to his sister, seemed apprehensive. The doctor said, "Don't be nervous, son. It will all be over before long." At that moment big tears welled up in the little boy's eyes. "Will I die pretty soon?" he asked. It then became apparent that he thought he was giving up his own life so that his baby sister might live!

Let love be without hypocrisy. Abhor that which is evil; cling to that which is good.   *Romans 12:9*

Some time ago a young sailor called his parents after his release from the military service. He said he was bringing his buddy home to stay with him. "You see, Mom," he said, "my friend is pretty badly broken up. He was severely wounded and has only one leg, one arm, and one eye." After a little reflection, the mother said grudgingly, "Of course, Son, I guess he can stay with us *a little while.*" Her voice, however, carried the message that they would not like to be burdened very long with such a severely handicapped fellow. Two days later they received a telegram from the admiral's office, saying their son had plunged to his death from a hotel window. When his body arrived for burial, his parents saw that he had only one arm, one leg, and one eye! The memory of her last conversation with him will linger with that mother as long as she lives. She often cries out, "Why didn't I speak more carefully, more lovingly? If only I could take back those thoughtless words 'he can stay with us *a little while.*' But it is too late now!"

Love suffereth long, and is kind; love envieth not;
love vaunteth not itself, is not puffed up, doth not
behave itself unseemly, seeketh not its own, is not
easily provoked, thinketh no evil, rejoiceth not in
iniquity, but rejoiceth in the truth.

1 Corinthians 13:4-6

An article appeared in the newspaper about a small boy who went to the lingerie department of a store to purchase a gift for his mother. Bashfully he told the clerk that he wanted to buy a slip for his mom, but he didn't know her size. The lady explained that it would help if he could describe her — was she thin, fat, short, tall, or what? "Well," replied the youngster, "she's just about perfect." So the clerk sent him home with a size 34. The news article followed up by reporting that a few days later the mother came to the store to exchange the gift. It was too small. She needed a size 52! The little fellow had seen her through the eyes of love, which didn't take into account the exact reading of the tape measure.

[Love] beareth all things, believeth all things,
hopeth all things, endureth all things.

1 Corinthians 13:7

A New England girl had just become engaged when the Civil War broke out. Her fiance was called into the army, so their wedding had to be postponed. The young soldier managed to get through most of the conflict without injury, but at the Battle of the Wilderness he was severely wounded. His bride-to-be, not knowing of his condition, read and reread his letters, counting the days until he would return. Suddenly the letters stopped coming. Finally she received one, but it was written in an unfamiliar handwriting. It read, "There has been another terrible battle. It is very difficult for me to tell you this, but I have lost both my arms. I cannot write myself, so a friend is writing this letter for me. While you are as dear to me as ever, I feel I should release you from the obligation of our engagement." The letter was never answered. Instead, the young woman took the next train and went directly to the place her loved one was being cared for. On arrival she found a sympathetic captain who gave her directions to her soldier's cot. Tearfully, she searched for her beloved. The moment she saw the young man, she threw her arms around his neck and kissed him. "I will never give you up!" she cried. "These hands of mine will help you; I will take care of you!"

And above all things have fervent love among yourselves; for love shall cover the multitude of sins. *1 Peter 4:8*

After reading the children's book *Little Lord Fauntleroy,* someone noted that it vividly illustrates the positive influence a person can have when he expresses a warm and trusting attitude toward others. The story is about a young boy of 7 who went to stay with his grandfather. Although the man had a reputation for being mean and selfish, the lad could see only the good in him. He said over and over again, "Grandpa, how people must love you! You're so good and kind in all you do." No matter how disagreeable the elderly man was, the grandson saw the best in everything he did. Finally, the youngster's unquestioning love softened the heart of the cantankerous old man. He couldn't resist the unwavering trust that the boy had in his goodness. As a result, he gradually began to change his ways, and in time he became the unselfish and kind person his grandson thought him to be.

Wherefore, I say unto thee, Her sins, which are many, are forgiven; for she loved much. But to whom little is forgiven, the same loveth little. *Luke 7:47*

A man who had been the superintendent of a city rescue mission for four decades was asked why he had spent his life working with dirty, unkempt, profane, drunken derelicts. He said, "All I'm doing is giving back to others a little of the love God has shown to me." As a young man, he himself had been a drunkard who went into a mission for a bowl of chili. There he heard the preacher say that Christ could save sinners, and he stumbled forward to accept the Lord Jesus as his Savior. Though his brain was addled by drink, he felt a weight lifted from his shoulders. That day he became a changed person. A little later, seeking God's will for his life, he felt the Lord calling him to go back to skid row and reach the people still wallowing there. The power of redeeming love enabled him to carry on his depressing task for 40 years.

He that despiseth his neighbor sinneth; but he that hath mercy on the poor, happy is he.

Proverbs 14:21

When Alfred the Great was defeated by the Danes, he retreated to a stronghold at Athelney. There a beggar came to his small castle and asked for food. The queen informed him that they had only one loaf of bread remaining, and that it was hardly sufficient for themselves. Then the king interrupted, "Give that poor man half of our bread. Our Lord, who could feed 5,000 with a few loaves and fishes, can certainly meet our needs with the half loaf that's left." The queen did as he instructed. This noble act of charity was not overlooked by the Lord. A few hours later a supply of fresh food arrived, sent by friends who knew of their impoverished condition.

For Further Study: Deuteronomy 10:19; Proverbs 17:9,17; Song of Solomon 8:6,7; Romans 13:8-10; Ephesians 5:2; 1 Peter 3:8.

Love for Enemies

But I say unto you that hear, Love your enemies, do
good to them who hate you, bless them that curse
you, and pray for them who despitefully use you.
Luke 6:27,28

During the Korean war, a young Communist officer ordered the execution of a Christian civilian. When he learned that his prisoner was in charge of an orphanage and was doing much good in caring for small children, he decided to spare his life but kill his son instead. The 19-year-old boy was shot in the presence of his father. When the tide of events changed, this same officer was captured, tried, and condemned to death for war crimes. Before the sentence could be carried out, however, the Christian father pleaded for the life of the Communist who had killed his son. He said that if justice were to be followed, this man would be executed. But since he was so young and blindly idealistic, he probably thought his actions were right. "Give him to me," he said, "and I'll teach him about the Savior." The request was granted, and the father took the murderer of his son into his own home. That remarkable demonstration of self-sacrificing love bore fruit, for that Communist became a Christian pastor!

And they stoned Stephen, calling upon God, and
saying, Lord Jesus, receive my spirit. And he
kneeled down, and cried with a loud voice, Lord,
lay not this sin to their charge. And when he had
said this, he fell asleep.   Acts 7:59,60

During the Revolutionary War, a faithful gospel preacher named Peter Miller lived near a man who hated him intensely for his Christian life and testimony. The fellow violently opposed him and ridiculed his followers. One day the unbeliever was found guilty of treason and sentenced to death. When he heard about this, Peter Miller set out on foot to intercede for the man's life before George Washington. The General listened to the minister's earnest plea, but told him he didn't feel he should pardon his friend. "My friend! He is not my friend," answered Miller. "In fact, he's my worst living enemy." "What!" said Washington. "You have walked 60 miles to save the life of your enemy? That, in my judgment, puts the matter in a different light. I will grant your request." With pardon in hand, Miller hurried to the place where his neighbor was to be executed, and arrived just as the prisoner was walking to the scaffold. When the traitor saw him, he exclaimed, "Old Peter Miller has come to have his revenge by watching me hang!" But he was astonished as he watched the minister step out of the crowd and produce the pardon which spared his life.

See that none render evil for evil unto any man, but ever follow that which is good, both among yourselves, and to all men.   *1 Thessalonians 5:15*

Two farmers lived side by side on land that was divided by a shallow river. On a day in August the cows belonging to one of them got out of the pasture, crossed the stream, and ruined about half an acre of the ripened corn that grew along the bank. The man who owned the field was so angry that he corralled his neighbor's cattle and locked them in his own barn. After making the first farmer pay for everything they had destroyed, he continued to hold the animals hostage until a high ransom was paid for them. In the fall of that year, some hogs belonging to the second farmer escaped through a broken fence, crossed the stream, and invaded the potato patch of the man who owned the cows. The pigs rooted around his property, grunting happily, and caused great damage. Although the man was disturbed by the loss of his crop, he carefully rounded up the strays and began herding them back to their own pen. When their owner saw him coming, he expected trouble and got out his gun. But he soon discovered that his neighbor had no intention of harming him or his hogs. Coming out of the place where he had been hiding, he said in surprise, "How can you be so kind to me after the way I treated you?" The man replied,

"Because I'm a Christian!" That evening the unsaved farmer and his wife paid a visit to the home of their good neighbor. Before they left, they had both accepted Christ—all because a consecrated believer refused to render "evil for evil."

Dearly beloved, avenge not yourselves but, rather, give place unto wrath; for it is written, Vengeance is mine; I will repay, saith the Lord.   *Romans 12:19*

During a time of terrible atrocities in Armenia, a young woman and her brother were being pursued down a street by a Turkish soldier. Cornering them, the armed man mercilessly shot the brother before the sister's eyes, then let her go free. Later, while she was working in a military hospital as a nurse, the soldier who had slain her brother was brought into her ward. He was critically wounded, and the slightest inattention to his needs would have meant certain death. When the nurse realized this, a terrible struggle took place in her mind. The old nature cried, "Vengeance!" But the Christ-life within whispered, "Kindness." She yielded to the Spirit's gentle prompting and patiently nursed him back to health. The Turk, who had recognized her, said to her one day, "Why didn't you let me die?" She replied simply, "I am a follower of Jesus, and He said, 'Love your enemies.' " The man was silent for a long time. At last he spoke. "I never knew that anyone could have such a faith. If that's what it does, tell me more about it. I want it."

Therefore, if thine enemy hunger, feed him; if he thirst, give him drink; for in so doing thou shalt heap coals of fire on his head. Be not overcome by evil, but overcome evil with good.
   Romans 12:20,21

A Christian lady owned two prize chickens that got out of their run and busied themselves in the garden of an ill-tempered neighbor. The man caught the hens, wrung their necks, and threw them back over the fence. Naturally, the woman was upset, but she didn't get angry and rush over and scream at him. Instead, she took the birds, dressed them, and prepared two chicken pies. Then she delivered one of the pies to the man who had killed her hens. She apologized for not being more careful about keeping her chickens in her own yard. Her children expected an angry scene, so they hid behind a bush to see the man's face and hear what he'd say. He was speechless! That chicken pie and apology filled him with shame. But the woman wasn't trying to get even. Her motive in returning good for evil was to show her neighbor true Christian love, and maybe even to bring him to faith in Christ.

For Further Study: Exodus 23:4,5; Proverbs 25:21,22; Matthew 5:44-48.

Marriage

Husbands, love your wives, and be not bitter
against them.   *Colossians 3:19*

A story is told about William Jennings Bryan, that great American orator and defender of the faith. As he was having his portrait painted, Bryan was asked, "Why do you wear your hair over your ears?" Bryan responded, "There is a romance connected with that. When I began courting Mrs. Bryan, she objected to the way my ears stood out. So to please her, I let my hair grow to cover them." "But that was many years ago," the artist said. "Why don't you have your hair cut now?" "Because," Bryan winked, "the romance is still going on."

But speak thou the things which become sound
doctrine: That the aged men be soberminded,
grave, temperate, sound in faith, in love, in
patience; the aged women likewise, that they be in
behavior as becometh holiness, not false accusers,

not given to much wine, teachers of good things, that
they may teach the young women to be sober-
minded, to love their husbands, to love their
children, to be discreet, chaste, keepers at home,
good, obedient to their own husbands, that the word
of God be not blasphemed.   *Titus 2:1-5*

A woman told psychologist George W. Crane that she hated her husband and wanted a divorce. "I want to hurt him all I can," she declared. "Well, in that case," said Dr. Crane, "I advise you to start showering him with compliments. When you have become indispensable to him, when he thinks you love him devotedly, then start the divorce action." The woman was intrigued by this novel approach. A few months later she returned and said that all was going well. "Good," said Dr. Crane, "now's the time to file for divorce." "Divorce?" she responded. "Never! I love my husband dearly."

Be ye not unequally yoked together with
unbelievers; for what fellowship hath
righteousness with unrighteousness? And what
communion hath light with darkness?
                              2 Corinthians 6:14

Olivia Langdon came from a Christian home. She fell in love with Mark Twain, a man who made no profession of faith in Christ. In spite of this, she married him. At first, her life made a deep impression upon him, and he regularly asked the blessing at mealtime and joined her in worship. But gradually this practice fell by the wayside, until one day he announced, "Livy, I don't believe in the Bible." In the months that followed, his unbelief subtly eroded her confidence in God. During a period of pressing sorrow, he tried to encourage her by saying, "Livy, if it comforts you to lean on the Christian faith, do so." But she could only reply, "Mark, I can't." Her once-vibrant faith had become too weak.

100

Thou shalt not covet thy neighbor's house; thou
shalt not covet thy neighbor's wife, nor his
manservant, nor his maidservant, nor his ox, nor
his ass, nor anything that is thy neighbor's.

Exodus 20:17

In *Benedicte's Scrapbook,* we read of a publisher who offered a prize for the best answer to the question, "Why is a newspaper like a good woman?" The winning answer was this: "It's like a good woman because every man should have one of his own and not look at his neighbor's!"

For Further Study: Genesis 2:18-25; Proverbs 18:22; Matthew 19:1-12; Matthew 22:23-30; Colossians 3:18,19; Hebrews 13:4.

Missions

And He said unto them, Go ye into all the world,
and preach the gospel to every creature.

Mark 16:15

After years of missionary service in South Africa, Robert Moffat returned to Scotland to recruit helpers. He traveled many miles one cold wintry night to speak at a church, but was dismayed that only a small group had come out to hear him. What bothered him even more was that the only people in attendance were ladies. Although he was grateful for their interest, he had hoped to challenge men. He had chosen as his text Proverbs 8:4, "Unto you, O men, I call." In his discouragement he almost failed to notice one small boy in the loft, pumping the bellows of the organ. Moffat felt frustrated as he gave his message, for he felt that very few women could be expected to undergo the rigorous life of the undeveloped jungle. But God works in mysterious ways. Although no one volunteered that evening, the young fellow assisting the organist was deeply moved by the challenge. As a result, he promised

God he would follow in the footsteps of this pioneer missionary. And he remained true to his vow. When he grew up, he devoted his life to carrying the gospel to the unreached tribes of Africa. His name was David Livingstone!

But ye shall receive power, after the Holy Spirit is come upon you; and ye shall be witnesses unto me both in Jerusalem, and in all Judea, and in Samaria, and unto the uttermost part of the earth.   *Acts 1:8*

A young woman was excited about her salvation and had a deep desire to share the gospel with others. So she asked her pastor where she might go to serve most effectively. He told her to come back the next day and he would have an answer for her. When she returned to his office at the specified time, the pastor handed her a folded slip of paper and said, "I'm suggesting someone who needs you right now more than anyone else in all the world." The young woman quickly left the pastor's study, eager to read where her mission field might be. When she opened the note, she discovered to her surprise that it bore these two words: "Your father." She had been so enthusiastic to reach the lost in distant lands that she had neglected someone close to home.

To the weak became I as weak, that I might gain the weak; I am made all things to all men, that I might by all means save some. And this I do for the gospel's sake, that I might be partaker of it with you.   *1 Corinthians 9:22,23*

A pastor and former missionary said, "I know something of the price of working for Christ in a savage land. Of the first 12 workers sent out by the Africa Inland Mission, I was the only one left after 30 months. I had been attacked by lions and rhinoceroses time and time again. I had been surrounded by warriors with bows and poisoned arrows, not knowing when they would shoot. For 14 months I never saw any bread, and for 2 months at one time I had to live on beans and sour milk. For weeks I was without the commonest of necessities, and I had to eat everything from ants to rhino. But in the superlative joy of that overwhelming experience—the joy of flashing the miracle-working Word of God into a great tribe that had never heard it before—I can never think of those 40 years in terms of sacrifice."

For they themselves show of us what manner of entering in we had unto you, and how ye turned to God from idols, to serve the living and true God.
                              1 Thessalonians 1:9

The story is told of a British earl who visited the Fiji Islands. Because he was an infidel, he critically remarked to an elderly chief, "You're a great leader, but it's a pity you've been taken in by those foreign missionaries. They only want to get rich through you. No one believes the Bible anymore. People are tired of hearing the threadbare story of Christ dying on the cross for the sins of mankind. They know better now. I'm sorry you've been so foolish as to accept their story." The old chief's eyes flashed as he answered, "See that great rock over there? On it we smashed the heads of our victims. Notice the furnace next to it. In that oven we formerly roasted the bodies of our enemies. If it hadn't been for those good missionaries and the love of Jesus that changed us from cannibals into Christians, you'd never leave this place alive! You'd better thank the Lord for the gospel; otherwise we'd already be feasting on you. If it weren't for the salvation message of the Bible, you'd now be our supper!"

Now there were in the church that was at Antioch certain prophets and teachers, as Barnabas, and Symeon, who was called Niger, and Lucius of Cyrene, and Manaen, who had been brought up

*with Herod, the tetrarch, and Saul. As they
ministered to the Lord, and fasted, the Holy Spirit
said, Separate Me Barnabas and Saul for the work
unto which I have called them. And when they had
fasted and prayed, and laid their hands on them,
they sent them away.*   Acts 13:1-3

An artist was asked to paint a picture of a decaying church. To the amazement of many, instead of depicting on canvas a tottering old building, he portrayed a stately edifice of modern design. Through open portals could be seen a richly carved pulpit, a magnificent organ, and beautiful stained-glass windows. In the vestibule was a large offering plate for the gifts of fashionable worshipers. But that's where the artist's idea of a decaying church became obvious. Next to this plate hung a small coinbox bearing an inscription that read, "For Foreign Missions." Over the slot through which contributions could be dropped he had painted a huge cobweb!

For Further Study: Psalm 96:3,10; Jonah 3:1-9;
Matthew 24:14; Matthew 28:19; Acts 10:9-20.

Obedience

*And Samuel said, Hath the Lord as great delight in
burnt offerings and sacrifices, as in obeying the
voice of the Lord? Behold, to obey is better than
sacrifice, and to hearken than the fat of rams.*
                                          1 Samuel 15:22

After a battle, an army captain was discussing the events of the day with his officers. He asked them which soldier in their opinion had been the most outstanding. Some of them mentioned a man who had died bravely; others suggested first one fighting man and then another. "No," said the captain, "you are all mistaken. The best man in the field today was a soldier who had lifted his arm to strike an enemy but dropped his arm without striking the blow the moment he heard the trumpeter sound retreat. That response to the general's command was the noblest thing done today."

For if any be a hearer of the word, and not a doer, he is like a man beholding his natural face in a mirror; for he beholdeth himself, and goeth his way, and immediately forgetteth what manner of man he was.
James 1:23,24

According to a UPI news report, a number of pamphlets entitled *The Control of Termites* was stored in the mailing room of a western university. Believe it or not, termites gobbled their way through the little booklets, and no one noticed until the damage was done. Those hungry little pests destroyed the information that could have prevented this from happening. All the facts contained in the leaflet didn't do a bit of good. Why? Because the knowledge was not applied!

For I spoke not unto your fathers, nor commanded them in the day that I brought them out of the land of Egypt, concerning burnt offerings or sacrifices; but this thing commanded I them, saying, Obey My voice, and I will be your God, and ye shall be My people; and walk in all the ways that I have commanded you, that it may be well unto you.
Jeremiah 7:22,23

The renowned preacher Donald Grey Barnhouse told of a missionary in Africa whose little son was playing in the yard. Suddenly he heard his father's voice. "Philip! Obey me instantly! Drop to the ground!" The boy did what he was told without any question. "Now crawl toward me as fast as you can." Again the boy obeyed. "Now stand up and run to me!" The lad followed instructions and ended in his father's arms. Only then did he look back at the tree where he had been playing. Hanging from a limb was a dangerous 15-foot snake! Suppose the boy had paused to ask why, or in a whining tone had inquired, "Do I have to do that right now?" He would have been killed by that deadly reptile. Barnhouse added, "Instant obedience is a mark of faith and love."

For Further Study: Exodus 19:5; Joshua 23:6,7; Psalm 119:1-8; Jeremiah 26:13; Acts 5:29.

Others

For the poor shall never cease out of the land;
therefore I command thee, saying, Thou shalt open
thine hand wide unto thy brother, to thy poor,
and to thy needy, in thy land.　　　*Deuteronomy 15:11*

A Christian named Tom was both ill and destitute. So John Wesley wrote him a comforting letter which read in part, "Dear Tom, I pray that you will soon be restored to health. 'Trust in the Lord, and do good; so shalt thou dwell in the land, and verily thou shalt be fed' " (Psalm 37:3). With the letter, Wesley enclosed a 5-pound note—a rather sizable sum in those days. Not long afterward he received this gracious reply from the man who had been blessed by his letter and his liberality: "Dear Brother Wesley, I have often been struck with the beauty of the Scripture passage you quoted, but I've never seen such a useful 'expository note' on it as the needed money you enclosed."

As we have, therefore, opportunity, let us do good
unto all men, especially unto them who are of the
household of faith.　　　*Galatians 6:10*

In an article in *Clear Horizons* comes this illustration of Christianity in action: "Sleet was falling and it was slushy underfoot. People hurried homeward with their coat collars up, hardly glancing at the others who passed by. A young man with a heavy satchel in one hand and a huge suitcase in the other was slipping and sliding as he rushed toward Grand Central Station. Suddenly a hand reached out and took one of his bags, and a pleasant voice said, 'Let me have that, Brother. In this bad weather, it's hard to carry so much!' At first the man was reluctant, but the smile of his would-be friend put him at ease. Soon they were walking together, chatting like two old buddies. Years later, Booker T. Washington said, 'That kindly deed was my introduction to Theodore Roosevelt.'"

For Further Study: Matthew 7:12; Romans 15:1,2; Galatians 6:1-5; Philippians 2:4.

Patience/Endurance

In your patience possess ye your souls.   Luke 21:19

From the *Choice Gleanings Calendar* comes the story of a judge who had been frequently ridiculed by a conceited lawyer. When asked by a friend why he didn't rebuke his assailant, he replied, "In our town lives a widow who has a dog. And whenever the moon shines, it goes outside and barks all night." Having said that, the magistrate shifted the conversation to another subject. Finally someone asked, "But Judge, what about the dog and the moon?" "Oh," he replied, "the moon went on shining—that's all."

And let us not be weary in well doing; for in due season we shall reap, if we faint not.   Galatians 6:9

Some of the greatest missionaries of history devotedly spread the seed of God's Word and yet had to wait long periods before seeing the fruit of their efforts. For example, William Carey labored 7 years before the first Hindu convert was brought to Christ in Burma, and Adoniram Judson toiled 7 years before his faithful preaching was rewarded. In West Africa, it was 14 years before one convert was received into the Christian church. In New Zealand, it took 9 years; and in

107

Tahiti, it was 16 years before the first harvest of souls began.

Wherefore, seeing we also are compassed about with so great a cloud of witnesses, let us lay aside every weight, and the sin which doth so easily beset us, and let us run with patience the race that is set before us.
                                                                Hebrews 12:1

The 19th-century Scottish minister George Matheson made the following observations about patience: "It is like the angel that guards the couch of an invalid who never complains, no matter how dark his valley. Yet, there is patience which is far more difficult—the patience that can run (Heb. 12:1). To lie down in time of grief, to be quiet under the stroke of adversity, implies a great faith; but nothing requires greater strength than to work. To have a heavy weight in our hearts and still to run the race; to have anguish in our spirits and still perform our daily tasks—that is Christlike in its character. The hardest thing is that most of us are called to exercise our patience, not in the sickbed, but in the busy street of activity."

For Further Study: Lamentations 3:26,27; 1 Thessalonians 5:14; Hebrews 10:36; James 1:2-4; James 5:7,8; 2 Peter 1:5,6.

Peace

Peace I leave with you, My peace I give unto you.
                                                                John 14:27

Matthew Henry had an interesting commentary on the peace the Lord Jesus gives. He wrote: "When Christ was about to leave this world, He made His will. His soul He committed to His Father; His body He bequeathed to Joseph to be decently interred; His clothes fell to the soldiers; His mother was left to the care of John. But what should He leave to His poor disciples? He had no silver or gold, but He left them that which was infinitely better—His peace!"

And who is he that will harm you, if ye be followers
of that which is good?   *1 Peter 3:13*

The truth of this verse is clearly illustrated in the experience of Bishop Berggrav of Norway. During the German occupation of his country in World War II, he was at his home with a friend when he heard a knock at the door. He opened it, and there was a German officer with a guard. They told him he was under arrest. Putting on his overcoat, he followed the soldiers to the waiting car. Just before it sped away, his friend called to him, "Remember 1 Peter 3:13." The bishop said he immediately reached into his pocket, pulled out a small Bible, and read the passage. As he did, he experienced an indescribable peace. He testified later that the reality of Christ's nearness came alive to him through this verse.

For Further Study: Psalm 4:8; Psalm 119:165; John 16:33; Romans 5:1; Romans 8:6; Galatians 5:22; Philippians 4:4-7.

Prayer

If any of you lack wisdom, let him ask of God, who
giveth to all men liberally, and upbraideth not, and
it shall be given him. But let him ask in faith,
nothing wavering. For he that wavereth is like a
wave of the sea driven with the wind and tossed.
James 1:5,6

Kara, a converted orphan girl, lived in a part of India where wickedness and spiritual darkness were prevalent. Fearing she would be made a slave and suffer abuse, she appealed to a visiting missionary who taught in another village to take her into her home. The sympathetic woman replied, "I'm sorry, but we have no vacant rooms and no money to build any." Kara tried to hold back the tears as she said, "O Missionary, please pray that God will let you take me, and I'll pray too." When the woman reached home that night, she found a letter from America with a large sum of money. Encouraged, she decided to use it to build an extra little room for the child who so badly needed a place to stay. The next morning she sent a helper to fetch Kara. She didn't expect them to return until late that night, for the journey was long. So she was surprised when the messenger came back with the young girl at noon. "When I prayed," the child said simply, "God assured me that it was His will for me to come to your home, so I thought I might as well get started." "She was almost here when I met her," said the missionary's helper with an approving smile.

Continue in prayer, and watch in the same with thanksgiving.　　　　　　　　　　　*Colossians 4:2*

When a missionary to Haiti returned to the United States, she reported a wonderful answer to prayer. She explained that during her most recent term on the field she had been told that she might have cancer. A biopsy was performed and sent away for analysis, but the medical report didn't come back for several weeks. As she waited for word, she could find no peace of mind. She recalled that she was afraid of what might happen to her husband and their small children. There seemed to be no relief to her distress. But one evening her anxiety suddenly lifted like a cloud. She had a deep and inexpressible awareness that the Lord would take care of the needs of her family, regardless of the outcome. Then it occurred to her that it was Wednesday evening—prayer meeting night back in the States. She also realized that it was the first Wednesday night after she and her husband had notified friends and supporters of their struggle. These facts convinced this faithful missionary couple that God had given them an opportunity to sense His answer to the prayers of others on their behalf. In addition, the medical report soon came back with the welcome news that there was no cancer.

I exhort, therefore, that first of all, supplications,
prayers, intercessions, and giving of thanks, be
made for all men, for kings, and for all that are in
authority, that we may lead a quiet and peaceable
life in all godliness and honesty.   *1 Timothy 2:1,2*

A Christian teacher devised a good way to remind her young students of the need for intercessory prayer. Holding up her arm, the woman explained, "When I am ready to pray, children, I look at my left hand. My thumb is the digit closest to me. This reminds me to pray for those near me—my family, my friends, my neighbors." Moving on, she touched her index finger and said, "When I was in school, my teacher always pointed this one at us. Preachers sometimes use it when they make a point or give a warning. So, as I come to this part of my hand, I pray for teachers, preachers, and others who have guided me." The children waited eagerly for her next comment. "My middle finger is my largest one. It stands above the others. This brings to my mind the rulers of our country and others in authority, and I pray for them. The fourth finger is the weakest. It makes me think of the helpless, the sick, and the poor. I ask the Lord to supply their needs and to strengthen them in body and soul." Coming to the little finger, she concluded, "This one stands for me, and so I finish by praying for myself and all the things that I need." The children never forgot that simple lesson.

And it shall come to pass that, before they call, I
will answer; and while they are yet speaking, I will
hear.   *Isaiah 65:24*

A widow, her young son, and her invalid daughter lived in a poor part of London. They had to move there because of the death of her husband and other problems that beset the family. The woman and her son went to a gospel meeting and they received the Savior. Friends in the church would gladly have helped them financially, but the family did not make their needs known.

111

The day came when their resources were exhausted and their meager income would stretch no further. That evening, while the mother and her son knelt in prayer beside the bed of the invalid daughter, this dear woman committed her need to God, being assured that His promises would never fail. The next morning the mailman delivered a letter. In the envelope was the equivalent of a week's wages. It had come from New Zealand and was sent by a total stranger. The benefactor had heard of the husband's death and had been moved to help the woman and her children. The letter had gone first to the village where they had lived, then it was forwarded to London. Five months after leaving New Zealand it finally arrived—the morning after the family prayer.

And whatever we ask, we receive of Him, because
we keep His commandments, and do those things
that are pleasing in His sight.   *1 John 3:22*

The captain of an ocean steamer told of one occasion when his ship was engulfed in a dense fog off the coast of Newfoundland. It was Wednesday evening, and the captain had been on the bridge for 24 hours when he was startled by someone tapping on his shoulder. He turned and saw one of his passengers—George Mueller. "Captain," said Mueller, "I must be in Quebec on Saturday afternoon." "That's impossible," replied the captain, "I'm helpless!" Mueller suggested, "Let's go down to the chart room and pray." The captain thought he had a lunatic on board. "Do you know how dense this fog is?" he asked. "No," came the reply, "my eye is not on the density of the fog, but on the living God who controls every circumstance of my life." Reluctantly the captain agreed to go with him to the chart room. When they arrived, Mueller got down on his knees and prayed, "O Lord, if it is consistent with Your will, please remove this fog in 5 minutes. You know the engagement You made for me in Quebec for Saturday. I believe it is Your will." Within minutes the fog lifted.

Draw near to God, and He will draw near to you.
Cleanse your hands, ye sinners; and purify your
hearts, ye double-minded. Be afflicted, and mourn,
and weep; let your laughter be turned to mourning,
and your joy to heaviness. Humble yourselves in the
sight of the Lord, and He shall lift you up.

James 4:8-10

Many years ago J. Wilbur Chapman wrote this to a friend: "I have learned some great lessons concerning prayer. At one of our missions in England the audience was exceedingly small, but I received a note saying that an American missionary was going to beseech the Lord on behalf of our work. The man was known as 'Praying Hyde.' Almost immediately the tide changed. Crowds began to pack the hall, and many accepted Christ as their Savior. Meeting Mr. Hyde later, I said, 'Brother, I want you to pray for me personally.' He came to my room, turned the key in the door, and dropped to his knees. He waited 5 minutes without a single syllable coming from his lips. I felt hot tears as they began running down my face. Although he had said nothing, I knew I was in the presence of God. Then with upturned face and with eyes streaming, he said, 'O God!' and was still again. When he seemed to sense that he was in full communion with the Lord, there came from the depths of his heart petitions such as I had never heard. I rose from my knees to know what real prayer was!"

Likewise, the Spirit also helpeth our infirmity; for
we know not what we should pray for as we ought;
but the Spirit Himself maketh intercession for us
with groanings which cannot be uttered.

Romans 8:26

The parable is told of two men who planted olive trees in their fields. Afterward one of them prayed, "Dear Lord, my trees need water. Please send rain." The showers came! He then petitioned, "They need sunshine," and God bathed them with sunlight! Later he cried, "Father, my trees need something to make them hardy. Please send a frost tonight." It came, but it killed them all. He went over to the other man's grove, and found that his olive trees were flourishing. "How can this be?" he asked. The reply came, "When I prayed, I didn't ask for rain, sunshine, or frost; I just said, 'Lord, you made these trees. You know what they need. Just send what is best!'"

Finally, brethren, pray for us, that the word of the Lord may have free course, and be glorified, even as it is with you.   *2 Thessalonians 3:1*

Five young college students were spending Sunday in London, so they went to hear C. H. Spurgeon preach. While waiting for the doors to open, the students were greeted by a man who said, "Gentlemen, let me show you around. Would you like to see the heating plant of this church?" They were not particularly interested, for it was a hot day in July. But they didn't want to offend the stranger, so they consented. The young men were taken down a stairway, a door was quietly opened, and their guide whispered, "This is our heating plant." Surprised, the students saw hundreds of people bowed in prayer, seeking a blessing on the service that was soon to begin in the auditorium above. Softly closing the door, the gentleman introduced himself. It was none other than Charles Spurgeon.

Pray without ceasing.   *1 Thessalonians 5:17*

A soldier was brought before his commanding officer and accused of communicating with the enemy. He had been seen emerging from an area where their troops were known to patrol. The poor man summed up his defense in a few words, stating that he had slipped away to spend an hour alone in prayer. "Have you been in the habit of spending an hour in private prayer?" demanded the officer. "Yes, sir," he replied. "Then," said his commander, "never in your life have you been

114

in more need of prayer than now. Kneel down and pray aloud so we all may hear you." Expecting the worst, the soldier dropped to his knees and poured out his heart to God. His prayer immediately revealed an intimacy with the Heavenly Father. His earnest fluency, his humble appeal for divine intervention, and his obvious trust in the One who is strong to deliver told unmistakably that he came regularly to the throne of grace. "You may go," said the officer. "No one could have prayed that way without a long apprenticeship; the fellows who never attend drill are always ill at ease for the review."

For Further Study: 1 Kings 8:22-30; Nehemiah 1:4-6; Psalm 145:18,19; Isaiah 55:1; Jonah 2:1,2,7; Matthew 6:5-13; Mark 11:24,25; Luke 11:13; John 15:7,16.

Reward

Blessed be the God and Father of our Lord Jesus Christ, who, according to His abundant mercy, hath begotten us again unto a living hope by the resurrection of Jesus Christ from the dead, to an inheritance incorruptible, and undefiled, and that fadeth not away, reserved in heaven for you, who are kept by the power of God through faith unto salvation ready to be revealed in the last time.

1 Peter 1:3-5

Henry C. Morrison often told of coming home from one of his many travels, having carried the message of the gospel to foreign lands. He arrived in New York aboard the same ship that brought President Theodore Roosevelt from one of his safaris in Africa. Thousands swarmed the docks to greet the illustrious hunter, but not a person was there to welcome Morrison. "Aha!" said the devil. "See how they greet the men of the world, and you—one of God's preachers—do not even have one person to meet you." He boarded the train for his home in Wilmore, Kentucky, and after several weary and lonely hours arrived at the station. No one from his family met him, for there had been a delay in information concerning his time of arrival. His heart ached as he rode alone in a hired carriage to his house. Humanly speaking, he had reason to complain; however, the Lord impressed upon him this thought: "Henry, you are not Home yet!"

His lord said unto him, Well done, good and faithful servant; thou hast been faithful over a few things, I will make thee ruler over many things. Enter thou into the joy of thy lord.
                                                        Matthew 25:23

One stormy night many years ago, an elderly couple entered the lobby of a small hotel and asked for a room. The clerk explained that because three conventions were in town, the hotel was filled. "But I can't send a nice couple like you out in the rain at 1 o'clock in the morning," he said. "Would you be willing to sleep in my room?" The couple hesitated, but the clerk insisted. The next morning, when the man paid his bill, he said, "You're the kind of manager who should be the boss of the best hotel in the United States. Maybe someday I'll build one for you." The clerk smiled, amused by the older man's "little joke." A few years passed. Then one day the clerk received a letter from the elderly man, re-calling that stormy night, and asking him to come to New York for a visit. A round-trip ticket was enclosed. When the clerk arrived, his host took him to the corner of 5th Avenue and 34th Street, where stood a magnificent new building. "That," explained the man, "is the hotel I have just built for you to manage." "You must be joking," said the clerk. "I most assuredly am not," came the reply. "Who—who are you?" stammered the other. "My name is William Waldorf Astor." That hotel was the original Waldorf-Astoria, and the young clerk who became its first manager was George C. Boldt.

For Further Study: Matthew 16:24-27; Luke 6:20-26,35; Luke 19:11-27.

Riches

Lay not up for yourselves treasures upon earth,
where moth and rust doth corrupt, and where
thieves break through and steal, but lay up for
yourselves treasures in heaven, where neither moth
nor rust doth corrupt, and where thieves do not
break through nor steal; for where your treasure is,
there will your heart be also.   *Matthew 6:19-21*

The story is told of a tax assessor who visited the home of a very poor citizen, a Christian, to appraise the value of his property. "I'm a rich man," said the believer. Surprised, the official reached for his pencil and prepared to make a long list of taxable items. He asked, "Well, what do you own?" The Christian replied, "I have a Savior who gave me everlasting life and who is preparing a place for me in the Eternal City." "What else?" asked the assessor. "I have a brave, godly wife and healthy, obedient, converted children." "Yes, and—?" "A merry heart that enables me to live joyfully." "Anything else?" "That's just the beginning." Realizing he was getting nowhere, the official closed his book, stood up, and concluded, "You are indeed a rich man, sir, but that kind of property is not subject to taxation."

For what shall it profit a man, if he shall gain the
whole world, and lose his own soul?   *Mark 8:36*

The British ship *Britannia* was wrecked off the coast of Brazil. Stored in the hold were many kegs filled with Spanish gold coins. The crew, hoping to save them, started to carry the barrels on deck. But the vessel was breaking up so fast that they had to abandon their efforts and rush for the lifeboats. Just before the last one pushed off, a young midshipman was sent back to see if anyone had been left behind. To his surprise, a man sat on the deck with a hatchet by his side. He had broken open a few kegs and was heaping up the gold around him. "What are you doing?" shouted the sailor. "Don't you know this ship is going to pieces?" "It may go down," said the man, "but I've lived in poverty all my life, and I am determined to die rich." All pleadings were brushed aside, and he was left to his fate.

For Further Study: 1 Samuel 2:7; Psalm 37:16; Proverbs 10:22; Proverbs 21:6; Proverbs 30:8,9; Ecclesiastes 5:9-20; Mark 4:19; 1 Timothy 6:6-10; 1 John 3:17.

Salvation

For whosoever shall call upon the name of the Lord shall be saved.   *Romans 10:13*

When Roy Gustafson visited Jamaica, he agreed to speak to the inmates of a large prison in Spanish Town. After singing and preaching the gospel to about 1,000 men, he received permission from a guard to talk to 14 convicts on death row. Gustafson realized that these men would never have another chance to hear the message of salvation. He whispered a silent prayer and began the meeting by singing Norman Clayton's beautiful gospel song, "Now I Belong to Jesus." He told them about his own conversion, and that he had turned his life over to God when he was only 18. One of the inmates, a 52-year-old murderer, was crouched in his cell, looking more like a wild beast than a man. Suddenly he cried out, "I'm going to die on Tuesday morning! Is there still hope for me?" "Oh, yes!" replied Gustafson. "The Bible says that 'whosoever shall call upon the name of the Lord shall be saved.'" Then he explained that Christ paid the debt of our sin, and that all we have to do is receive Him. The convict knelt on the dirty floor and sobbed openly as he asked the Savior to forgive him. Then, smiling through his tears, he pleaded, "Sing it again!" Once more Gustafson repeated those assuring words: "Now I belong to Jesus, Jesus belongs to me—not for the years of time alone, but for eternity." On Tuesday morning that converted murderer went to the gallows singing those same comforting words.

But as many as received Him, to them gave He power to become the children of God, even to them that believe on His name.　　　　　*John 1:12*

William McCarrell often used the following story to point out what a person has to do to be saved: "While Andrew Jackson was President of the United States, a man was given a court trial and was condemned to die. President Jackson offered to pardon him, but the condemned man refused the pardon. Prison authorities, the Attorney General, and others tried to convince the man to accept the pardon. They sought to impress upon him that if he did not accept the pardon, he would be insulting the President of the United States. The man persisted. The Attorney General consulted the Supreme Court, asking if legal authorities could force the man to receive the pardon. The court ruled that the pardon was merely a printed statement until the man accepted it. If he rejected the pardon, it remained printed matter."

He raiseth up the poor out of the dust, and lifteth the needy out of the dunghill that He may set him with princes, even with the princes of His people.　　　　*Psalm 113:7,8*

In the early days of the American frontier, an Indian chief heard the message of the gospel and was gloriously saved. Such an indescribable peace flooded his soul that he couldn't keep from talking about the Lord. Another chief visited him and wanted to know who this Jesus was, what He had done, and where He lived. The convert took some chips of wood, made a small circle on the ground, and put a worm in the center. Then he set the wood on fire. The little creature tried to get out of the ring of flame, vainly seeking a way of escape. The converted Indian suddenly lifted the worm out of the place of ever-increasing danger, saying, "That prison of flame is this world, and I was like that worm. The powers of sin and evil surrounded me, and I was helpless to save myself. Then the Great Chief, the Lord Jesus Christ, came down from heaven right into this circle of death, lifted me out of the fire of sin and hell, and made me His child."

And we have seen and do testify that the Father sent the Son to be the Savior of the world.   *1 John 4:14*

At the close of a Sunday service, a stranger came up to Pastor D. M. Stearns and informed him that he was displeased with the message he had just delivered. "I don't care for your preaching, Dr. Stearns," he said. "I don't care for the cross. I think that instead of preaching the death of Christ, it would be far better to preach about Jesus as the teacher and example." "Would you be willing to follow Him if I preached that way?" asked the minister. "I would," said the stranger, "I would follow in His steps." "Then let us take the first step. It is said of Him that He 'did no sin' (1 Peter 2:22). Can you take that step?" The man looked confused. "No," he said, "I do sin, and I acknowledge it." "Well then," said Dr. Stearns, "your first need of Christ is not as an example but as a Savior. You must have His Spirit to guide you before you can walk 'in His steps.' "

For Christ also hath once suffered for sins, the just for the unjust, that He might bring us to God, being put to death in the flesh but made alive by the Spirit.   *1 Peter 3:18*

The *Gray and Adams Commentary* tells the story of Kazinak, a wicked chieftain in Greenland. One day he stormed into a hut where a missionary was translating the gospel of John and demanded to know what he was doing. The man explained that the marks he was making were words, and that they came from a book that could speak. Kazinak asked what it said, so the missionary read the account of Christ's death. The chief immediately wanted to know, "What has this Man done? Has He robbed anybody? Has He murdered anybody?" "No," was the reply. "Then why does He suffer? Why must He die?" "Listen," said the missionary, "this Man has done no wrong, but Kazinak has done wrong. This Man has robbed no one, but Kazinak has robbed many. This Man has murdered no one, but Kazinak has murdered his brother. This Man suffered that Kazinak might not suffer; He died that Kazinak might not die." "Tell me that again!" said the astonished chieftain. This wicked man was hearing the gospel for the first time. He recognized his own sinfulness and the sinlessness of Christ, and that day he accepted Him as his Savior.

Therefore, if any man be in Christ, he is a new creation; old things are passed away; behold, all things are become new.   *2 Corinthians 5:17*

One Sunday in Chicago, some professional baseball players were leaving a saloon when they saw a crowd gathered on the sidewalk. They were watching a group from the Pacific Garden Mission as they played instruments, sang gospel hymns, and testified of Christ's power to save. Harry Monroe gave a brief message. One of the men was deeply moved as boyhood memories raced through his mind. He thought of his godly mother praying for him and of the old church he had attended. With tears in his eyes he said, "Boys, I'm through! I'm going to turn from my sin and come to Christ. I guess it's hard for you to understand, but we've come to a parting of the ways." Some mocked him, while others stood in stunned silence. He went to the Mission and there called upon God for mercy. Later he testified, "I staggered out of my sins into the outstretched arms of the Savior. I instantly became a new creature in Him!" That ballplayer's name was Billy Sunday.

This is a faithful saying, and worthy of all
acceptance, that Christ Jesus came into the world
to save sinners, of whom I am chief.   *1 Timothy 1:15*

An interesting thing happened one day in the church where Samuel Colgate, the great American businessman, was a member. During an evangelistic campaign a prostitute came forward and confessed her sins. She was brokenhearted and wept openly. She asked God to save her soul, and she expressed her desire to join the church. "I'll gladly sit in some back corner," she said. The preacher hesitated to call for a motion to accept her into membership, and for a few moments the silence was oppressive. Finally, a member stood up and suggested that action on her request be postponed. At that point Mr. Colgate arose and said with an undertone of sarcasm, "I guess we blundered when we prayed that the Lord would save sinners. We forgot to specify what kind. We'd better ask Him to forgive us for this oversight. The Holy Spirit has touched this woman and made her truly repentant, but apparently the Lord doesn't understand that she isn't the type we want Him to rescue." Many in the audience blushed with shame. They had been guilty of judging like the Pharisee in the temple who exclaimed self-righteously, "God, I thank Thee that I am not as other men are, extortioners, unjust, adulterers" (Luke 18:11). Another motion was made, and the woman was unanimously received into the fellowship.

And they said, Believe on the Lord Jesus Christ,
and thou shalt be saved, and thy house.

Acts 16:31

Abraham Lincoln was a great man and a great President. But many do not know that he was not saved until the last few months of his life. Some years ago, *Moody Monthly* pointed this out in an interesting article. It stated: "Abraham Lincoln was raised in a fine Christian home. He once said of his mother, 'I remember her prayers and they have always followed me.' In his youth, Lincoln showed great interest in the

Bible and spiritual truths. He memorized large portions of Scripture and read such works as *Pilgrim's Progress*. As an adult, however, he strayed from his godly training. But with the burdens of the Civil War pressing down upon him, President Lincoln began to experience a change of heart. Not long before he was killed, he was asked, 'Do you love Jesus?' He replied, 'When I left Springfield, I asked the people to pray for me. But I was not a Christian! When I buried my son, the severest trial of my life, I still was not a Christian. But at Gettysburg I consecrated myself to Christ. Yes, I now can truly say I do love Jesus!' "

Marvel not that I said unto thee, Ye must be born again.   *John 3:7*

The truth of this promise is vividly portrayed in the life of George Whitefield. At the age of 16, he became deeply convicted of his sin. He tried everything possible to erase his guilt through religious activity. He wrote, "I fasted for 36 hours twice a week. I prayed formal prayers several times a day and almost starved myself to death during Lent, but I only felt more miserable. Then by God's grace I met Charles Wesley, who gave me a book that showed me from the Scriptures that I must be born again or be eternally lost." Finally, by the work of the Holy Spirit in his heart, Whitefield came to understand Jesus' words in John 3. He believed and was gloriously saved. After he became a preacher, he spoke at least a thousand times on the subject, "Ye must be born again." He fervently desired that all who heard him might experience for themselves the transforming power of God's grace.

Neither is there salvation in any other; for there is no other name under heaven given among men, whereby we must be saved.   *Acts 4:12*

Shortly after D. L. Moody was converted, he was visiting a town in Illinois, where the wife of a judge begged him to call on her infidel husband. The inexperienced evangelist replied, "I'm afraid I can't talk to him. I'm just a new Christian." When she insisted, however, Moody went to see him. Their conversation was short. "Judge," he said, "I can't reason with a man like you, for I have no learning. I can only tell you that you must believe on the Lord Jesus Christ to be saved. If you are ever converted, I want you to be sure to let me know." The judge replied, "Young man, if such an unlikely thing happens, you'll certainly hear about it." Remarkably, the judge was saved within a year; and, true to his word, he wrote to tell Moody how it happened. "One night while my wife was at a prayer meeting, I began to grow very uneasy and miserable. This distress lasted throughout the night, and the next morning I was not able to eat my breakfast. When I got to the office, I told the employees to take the day off, and then I shut myself up in a small room where I wouldn't be disturbed. In desperation I got down on my knees and began praying over and over again, 'God, forgive my sins,' but no answer came. I couldn't get myself to say 'for Jesus sake,' because I didn't believe in the atonement. But at last I cried, 'O God, in the name of the Lord Jesus, forgive my sins!' Immediately I found peace."

For Further Study: Psalm 32; Matthew 1:21;
Matthew 21:28-32; Luke 15:11-32; Acts 9:1-9; Romans 4.

Sanctification

I am crucified with Christ: nevertheless I live; yet not I, but Christ liveth in me; and the life which I now live in the flesh I live by the faith of the Son of God, who loved me and gave Himself for me.
Galatians 2:20

When fourth century scholar Augustine was still without God and without hope, the Holy Spirit convicted him on the basis of Paul's words in Romans 13:14,

"But put ye on the Lord Jesus Christ, and make not provision for the flesh, to fulfill its lusts." Augustine acknowledged his sinfulness, accepted Jesus as his Savior, and became a different person. His entire outlook on life began to change because of his new nature. One day he had to attend to some business in his old haunts in Rome. As he walked along, a former companion recognized him and called out, "Augustine, Augustine, it is I." He took one look at the poor, disreputable woman whose company he had formerly enjoyed, and he shuddered. Reminding himself of his new position in Christ, he turned and ran from her, shouting, "It's not I! It's not I!" Augustine had found the secret of Paul's words: "I live; yet not I, but Christ liveth in me" (Gal. 2:20).

I beseech you therefore, brethren, by the mercies of God, that ye present your bodies a living sacrifice, holy, acceptable unto God, which is your reasonable service.   *Romans 12:1*

Several years ago I read an article about Queen Mary, who made it her practice to visit Scotland every year. She was so loved by the people there that she often mingled with them freely without a protective escort. While walking with some children one afternoon, she went out farther than she had planned. Dark clouds came up unexpectedly, so she stopped at a nearby house to borrow an umbrella. "If you will lend me one," she said to the lady who answered the door, "I will send it back to you tomorrow." The woman didn't recognize the Queen and was reluctant to give this stranger her best umbrella. So she handed her one that she intended to throw away. The fabric was torn in several places and one of the ribs was broken. The next day another knock was heard at the door. When the woman opened it, she was greeted by a royal guard, who was holding her old, tattered umbrella. "The Queen sent me," he said. "She asked me to thank you for loaning her this." For a moment the woman was stunned, then she burst into tears. "Oh, what an opportunity I missed," she cried. "I didn't give the Queen my very best!"

For ye are the temple of the living God; as God hath said, I will dwell in them, and walk in them; and I will be their God, and they shall be My people.
2 Corinthians 6:16

When Queen Victoria reigned in England, she occasionally would visit some of the humble cottages of her subjects. One time she entered the home of a widow and stayed to enjoy a brief period of Christian fellowship. Later on, the poor woman was taunted by her worldly neighbors. "Granny," they said, "who's the most honored guest you've ever entertained in your home?" They expected her to say it was Jesus, for despite their constant ridicule of her Christian witness, they recognized her deep spirituality. But to their surprise she answered, "The most honored guest I've entertained is Her Majesty the Queen." "Did you say the Queen? Ah, we caught you this time! How about this Jesus you're always talking about? Isn't He your most honored guest?" Her answer was definite and scriptural. "No indeed! He's not a guest. HE LIVES HERE!"

The Spirit Himself beareth witness with our spirit, that we are the children of God; and if children, then heirs— heirs of God, and joint-heirs with Christ—if so be that we suffer with Him, that we may be also glorified together. Romans 8:16,17

The royal parents of Princess Victoria felt that she should be told early in life that someday she might become Queen of England. They instructed her governess to make this known to her. So she inserted in the girl's history textbook a list of the Hanoverian kings. At the end of the column she had written the name "Victoria." The tutor watched closely as the Princess studied her lesson. When Victoria read down the page

126

and came to her own name, she looked up and said, "Can it really be that I may become the Queen of England?" The governess replied, "Yes, in all probability you will." After a pause, the princess said thoughtfully, "Then, I will be good!"

Blessed are the pure in heart; for they shall see God.
Matthew 5:8

In the forests of Northern Europe lives the ermine, a small animal best known for his snow-white fur. Instinctively, he protects his glossy coat with great care lest it become soiled. Hunters often capitalize on this trait. Instead of setting a mechanical trap to catch the ermine, they find his home in a cleft of a rock or a hollow tree and daub the entrance and the interior with tar. Then their dogs start the chase, and the frightened ermine flees toward his home. But finding it covered with dirt, he spurns the place of safety. Rather than soil his white fur, he courageously faces the yelping dogs, who hold him at bay until the hunters capture him. To the ermine, purity is dearer than life!

For Further Study: Jeremiah 1:5; John 17:17,19; 1 Corinthians 1:2,30; 1 Corinthians 6:11; 1 Thessalonians 4:3,4; Hebrews 10:1-18.

Satan

Put on the whole armor of God, that ye may be able to stand against the wiles of the devil.
Ephesians 6:11

Nature provides an analogy that reminds us of the insidious tactics employed by our adversary. According to scientists, Arctic polar bears feed almost entirely on seals. To capture a meal, they sometimes resort to a cunning bit of trickery. If the hole through which the seal gets his food is near the edge of the ice, the polar bear will take a deep breath and swim under the water to its exact location. He will then imitate a fish by making a tiny scratching sound on the underside of the ice. When the hungry seal hears this, he dives in for a quick supper, only to find himself suddenly entrapped in the powerful embrace of his huge predator.

But I fear, lest by any means, as the serpent beguiled Eve through his craftiness, so your minds should be corrupted from the simplicity that is in Christ.   *2 Corinthians 11:3*

The moment someone mentions a chameleon, we immediately think of its ability to change color and blend into the environment. But this little lizard has some other unusual characteristics as well. Those two bulging eyes, for example, can look in different directions at the same time. And if it exerts itself and needs extra support, it can coil its tail around a branch, thus giving it a "fifth leg." But that's not all. A chameleon can extend its tongue almost a foot to catch an insect. Because of a sticky substance on the end of its tongue, anything it touches is instantly entrapped. All the while, the chameleon is practicing his deceptive art of camouflage. Satan engages in a similar kind of craftiness. He's the master of deceit.

And the servant of the Lord must not strive, but be gentle unto all men, apt to teach, patient, in meekness instructing those that oppose him, if God, perhaps, will give them repentance to the acknowledging of the truth, and that they may recover themselves out of the snare of the devil, who are taken captive by him at his will.
                         2 Timothy 2:24-26

Monkey trappers in North Africa have a clever method of catching their prey. A number of gourds are filled with nuts and firmly fastened to a branch of a tree. Each has a hole just large enough for the unwary monkey to stick his forepaw into it. When the hungry animal discovers this cache of food, he reaches in and grabs a handful. But the hole is too small for him to

128

withdraw his clenched fist, and he doesn't have enough sense to open his paw and let go. Thus he is easily taken captive.

For Further Study: Job 1:12; Job 2:6; Isaiah 14:12-20; Ezekiel 28:12-19; Matthew 4:1-11; John 8:44; Revelation 12:9.

Second Coming

For the Lord Himself shall descend from heaven with a shout, with the voice of the archangel, and with the trump of God; and the dead in Christ shall rise first; then we who are alive and remain shall be caught up together with them in the clouds, to meet the Lord in the air; and so shall we ever be with the Lord.   *1 Thessalonians 4:16,17*

A man in Cheshire, England, sent Radio Bible Class a thoughtful letter that included these comments: "Several years ago on Christmas Eve, my wife had tucked our 10-year-old twins in their beds and had settled down for a quiet time with the Lord by the fire in the living room. Suddenly she was startled by the sound of music just outside our front door, followed almost immediately by the excited voice of our daughter Carol crying, 'Mommy, Mommy, Jesus is here!' The youngster came rushing down the stairs in her nightgown, her face bright with expectation as she awaited the joyous moment of meeting the Savior. My wife kissed her and gently ushered her back to bed, explaining that the clear, sweet notes she had heard were not made by the 'trump of God' (1 Thessalonians 4:16). Rather, they were part of a stirring horn fanfare being sounded out by the Salvation Army Band as they came down our garden path to play Christmas carols for us. Yet, what a lesson that moment of excitement provided for us! To see the glowing face of our child, eagerly looking for her Lord to come, was a sermon in itself!"

For Further Study: Matthew 24:29-35; Mark 13:32-37; John 14:3; Acts 1:1-11; Titus 2:11-14.

Service

*After that He poureth water into a basin, and began
to wash the disciples' feet, and to wipe them with the
towel with which He was girded.*   John 13:5

In her book *The Mark Of A Man,* Elisabeth Elliot
gave an excellent illustration of leading by serving.
She told of a relative who was the dean of a Christian
college in the Midwest. One night some boys in a dorm
had been rowdy, smearing the walls with shaving
cream, peanut butter, and jelly. When the dean heard
about it, he wondered what action he should take. He
could force the young men to clean it up, or he could
order the janitor to do it. Instead, he went to a closet,
filled a bucket with soapy water, and began to clean up
the mess himself. Soon doors began to open, and before
long the guilty ones were helping him wash the walls.
Because he was willing to take the role of a servant, he
solved the problem and taught the boys a valuable
lesson at the same time.

*And Jesus, immediately knowing in Himself that
power had gone out of Him, turned about in the
crowd, and said, Who touched My clothes? And His
disciples said unto Him, Thou seest the multitude
crowding Thee, and sayest Thou, Who touched Me?
And He looked round about to see her that had
done this thing. But the woman, fearing and
trembling, knowing what was done in her, came
and fell down before Him, and told Him all the
truth. And He said unto her, Daughter, thy faith
hath made thee well. Go in peace, and be well of thy
plague.*   Mark 5:30-34

In the 1890s, a quaint newspaper named *The Ram's
Horn* attracted a loyal following with its fine collection
of epigrams and anecdotes. It once recounted that
Julia Ward Howe, in her efforts to free slaves, had
asked a United States senator to help liberate a black
man from a desperate situation. The legislator ex-

claimed, "Madam, I'm so busy with plans for the benefit of the whole race that I have no time to help individuals!" Angered by his lack of compassion, Mrs. Howe replied, "I'm glad our Lord never displayed such a calloused attitude!"

And whosoever shall give to drink unto one of these little ones a cup of cold water only in the name of a disciple, verily I say unto you, he shall in no way lose his reward.   *Matthew 10:42*

The Queen of England was visiting Canada, and the town where she was staying had been deluged with rain. Seeing a muddy place in the pathway where the royal guest was to tread, a gallant young man removed his raincoat in the tradition of Sir Walter Raleigh and spread it over the puddle. The Queen gave him a grateful smile of recognition, but she took a slight detour to avoid the spot he had so graciously covered. The press, taking note of this incident, blazoned the young man's name across the front page of many newspapers around the world. It was not the greatness of the deed but the one for whom it was performed that made it noteworthy!

And it came to pass, when the time was come that He should be received up, He steadfastly set His face to go to Jerusalem, and sent messengers before His face; and they went, and entered into a village of the Samaritans, to make ready for Him. And they did not receive Him, because His face was as though He would go to Jerusalem.   *Luke 9:51-53*

A gifted young man named George returned home from college and was asked by his Sunday school superintendent to teach a class. He promptly declined. When the pastor urged him to accept the challenge, he nonchalantly remarked, "There's no penalty for refusing, is there?" "Yes, there certainly is," said the minister.

131

"It's the penalty of not knowing what God could have accomplished through your life if you had obeyed Him." "If I don't know about it," said George flippantly, "I guess I won't miss it." The pastor then inquired, "Do you remember the incident in Jesus' life when a Samaritan village would not receive Him? Some of His disciples wanted to call down fire and brimstone as a punishment, but Jesus rebuked them and patiently resumed His journey. What do you think it cost the people of that little town because they refused to serve the Lord?" "I don't recall any penalty. As far as I know, nothing ever happened to them," replied George. "You're right," the minister agreed. "The people went to bed as usual. The next morning they got up, and nothing out of the ordinary occurred. No sick were healed, no parable was spoken, and no disciples were called. Had Jesus performed some miracle or taught in that village, it would have had a prominent place in history because of the good accomplished there. Instead, even its name is unknown." For a moment George was silent. Then he said, "Thank you, Pastor, for your advice. I'll teach that class!"

Also I heard the voice of the Lord, saying, Whom shall I send, and who will go for us? Then said I, Here am I; send me.　　　　　　　　*Isaiah 6:8*

The Ashanti tribe of West Africa proclaimed war against the British crown in 1823. A small body of government troops was soon overrun by the rebels, resulting in the death of the governor of the colony and almost all of his officers. This, of course, stirred the wrath of the Britons, and in another engagement in 1826 the Ashantis were completely defeated near Accra. During that campaign a commander announced to his regiment that a number of men were needed for a hazardous undertaking. They were told that it might mean the death of all who would participate, yet it was a mission urgently requested by their king. The officer said, "Every man who cares to volunteer, let him step one pace forward!" He turned on his heel for a moment to give them time to make the decision. Then swinging around again, he was amazed to find the line unbroken. "What?" he cried. "Will no one offer to serve?" "Begging your pardon, sir," said one, "the whole line has volunteered!"

So ye also, when ye shall have done all those things which are commanded you, say, We are unprofitable servants; we have done that which was our duty to do.   *Luke 17:10*

A good example of right attitude in serving was manifested by David Livingstone. Even with all his accomplishments he is quoted as saying, "People talk of the sacrifice I have made in spending so much of my life in Africa. Can that be called a sacrifice which simply pays back a small part of the great debt we owe God? Is anything a sacrifice when it brings its own blessed reward in healthful activity, consciousness of doing good, peace of mind, and a bright hope of a glorious destiny hereafter? Away with such a thought! It's not a sacrifice, it's a privilege."

Verily, verily, I say unto you, Except a grain of wheat fall into the ground and die, it abideth alone; but if it die, it bringeth forth much fruit.
                                              John 12:24

A Christian who was born and raised in a log house had a deep longing to return to his humble boyhood home. He had been away for 35 years, so he was glad when he had an opportunity to visit that cherished place. As he walked across the yard, observing the now-deserted cabin, he remembered that as a youngster he had planted some walnuts along a stream that ran through his father's farm. When he went down to the creek, he discovered a beautiful row of stately walnut trees. Then he recalled that he had also hidden some nuts in the attic of the old cabin. He was curious to see what had happened to them, so he climbed into the dark attic and poked around in a corner until he found them. What a difference! Those he had stored were

133

nothing but dry and dust-covered nuts, while the ones he had planted had become flourishing green trees. Immediately the words of the Lord Jesus came to his mind with new meaning, "Except a grain of wheat fall into the ground and die, it abideth alone; but if it die, it bringeth forth much fruit."

For we are laborers together with God; ye are God's cultivated field, ye are God's building.
                                                    1 Corinthians 3:9

The following parable illustrates the truth found in 1 Corinthians 3:9. It seems the carpenter's tools were having a conference. Brother Hammer was presiding, but the others informed him that he would have to leave because he was too noisy. "All right," he said, "I'll go, but Brother Plane must withdraw too. There's no depth to his work. It's always on the surface." Brother Plane responded, "Well, Brother Rule will also have to go. He's constantly measuring people as if he were the only one who's right." Brother Rule complained about Brother Sandpaper, saying, "He's rougher than he ought to be. He's always rubbing people the wrong way." In the midst of the discussion, the Carpenter of Nazareth walked in. He went to His workbench to make a pulpit from which to preach the gospel. He used the hammer, the plane, the rule, and the sandpaper. After the pulpit was finished, Brother Rule arose and said, "I see now that all of us are laborers together with God."

For Further Study: Luke 10:39-42; Ephesians 6:5-8; Philippians 2:19-30.

Sin

For all have sinned, and come short of the glory of God.   *Romans 3:23*

Many years ago in Waterbury, Connecticut, a black evangelist wanted to emphasize the truth that men are

134

"dead in trespasses and sins" (Eph. 2:1). The overflow crowd at the African Methodist Church one Sunday morning was shocked to see a casket covered with flowers in front of the pulpit. They were even more amazed when the evangelist gave a graphic description of hell and all of its horrors. As he dwelt on the darkness, isolation, pain, and remorse experienced by the soul that is eternally separated from God, some in the congregation began to weep and tremble. The preacher said he found it impossible to eulogize the dead person, for he had committed grievous sins that deserved only God's wrath. "The one you will soon view is justly condemned to eternal torment," he said. At the end of his sermon the flowers were removed from the coffin and the audience was asked to walk past the casket, keeping about 10 feet apart. They were to look once at this horrible sinner and then return to their seats in silence. Each person peered fearfully into the casket, but found it empty. However, a full-length mirror in the bottom reflected his own face as he stared in amazement. In the closing moments of the service, the solemn and convicted audience was reminded that although sin brings the penalty of death, the gift of God through Christ provides a way of escape.

Who can bring a clean thing out of an unclean?
Not one.   *Job 14:4*

On August 16, 1952, a proud new father called a press conference in a Brooklyn hospital. To the few reporters who showed up he said, "Meet my daughter Edith. She's going to be a genius. I shall make her into the perfect human being." During the years that followed, the man and his daughter astounded educators and the press with their experiment. When she entered school at the age of 6, she was reading two books a day along with the *New York Times*. Later she scored consistently around 200 on an IQ scale that rated 150 as genius. At age 24, the woman was interviewed by a reporter. One of the questions asked was whether she felt that her father had created the perfect human being. Her reply was revealing: "How can imperfection create perfection? . . . I'm sitting here overweight, having withdrawal symptoms from something as silly as cigarettes, and wishing I had something sweet to stick in my mouth, and you're asking me if I'm perfect."

> *But exhort one another daily, while it is called*
> *Today, lest any of you be hardened through the*
> *deceitfulness of sin.*   *Hebrews 3:13*

Popular evangelist J. Wilbur Chapman told of a preacher friend who delivered a powerful sermon on the subject of sin. After the service, one of the church officers confronted the minister in his study and offered what he thought was some needed counsel. "Pastor," he said, "we don't want you to talk as openly as you do about man's guilt and corruption. If our boys and girls hear you discussing that subject, they will more easily become sinners. Call it a mistake if you want to, but do not speak so plainly about sin." The pastor removed a small bottle from a shelf behind his desk. Showing it to the man, he said, "You see this label? It says 'Strychnine,' and underneath in bold, red letters is the word 'POISON.' What you are asking me to do would be like changing this label. Suppose I write over it 'Essence of Peppermint.' Someone who doesn't know the danger might use it and become very ill. The milder the label, the more dangerous the poison!"

> *I acknowledged my sin unto Thee, and mine*
> *iniquity have I not hidden. I said, I will confess my*
> *transgressions unto the Lord, and Thou forgavest*
> *the iniquity of my sin.*   *Psalm 32:5*

The story is told that one day Frederick the Great, King of Prussia, visited a prison and talked with each of the inmates. There were endless tales of innocence, of misunderstood motives, and of exploitation. Finally the king stopped at the cell of a convict who remained silent. "Well," remarked Frederick, "I suppose you are an innocent victim too?" "No, sir, I'm not," replied the man. "I'm guilty, and I deserve my punishment." Turning to the warden, the king said, "Here! Release this rascal before he corrupts all the fine innocent people in this place!"

But He was wounded for our transgressions, He was bruised for our iniquities; the chastisement for our peace was upon Him, and with His stripes we are healed. Isaiah 53:5

A man who was deeply troubled by his sins had a vivid dream in which he saw Jesus being savagely whipped by a soldier. As the cruel scourge came down upon Christ's back, the dreamer shuddered, for the terrible instrument left gaping wounds upon the bleeding, swollen body of the Savior. When the soldier raised his arm to strike the Lord again, the dreamer rushed forward to stop him. As he did, the one who wielded the lash turned—and the startled dreamer recognized himself! He awoke in a cold sweat, realizing that his sin had brought this grievous punishment upon the Savior.

But every man is tempted, when he is drawn away of his own lust, and enticed. Then when lust hath conceived, it bringeth forth sin; and sin, when it is finished, bringeth forth death. James 1:14,15

A tragedy occurred in England some years ago when a noted circus performer was attacked by one of his trained animals. E. G. Clark gave this eyewitness account: "After the man had shown his complete mastery over several lions, tigers, leopards, and hyenas, he concluded his act by introducing an enormous boa constrictor nearly 30 feet long. He had bought the reptile when it was only 2 or 3 days old, and for 25 years had handled it daily so that he considered it perfectly harmless and completely under his control. As the huge serpent slithered along, its head erect, its bright eyes sparkling, the entertainer gave a prearranged signal to the powerful creature. As it had done every day before, it began to coil its heavy folds around him. Higher and higher it rose until the man and the serpent seemed blended into one, and the hideous head of the snake was raised above his own. Suddenly the trainer gave a muffled cry, and the audience burst into applause. Their cheers froze on their lips, however, for it soon became obvious that the man's scream was a death wail of agony. Without warning, the boa constrictor's serpent-nature had returned, and its shiny, rippling body embraced him for the last time. The crowd heard bone after bone crack as the killer tightened its hold. The man's plaything had become his master and destroyer."

For God sent not His Son into the world to condemn the world, but that the world through Him might be saved.   *John 3:17*

A barber and a minister were walking through the city slums. The barber, who was an atheist, remarked, "This is why I cannot believe in a God of love. If He is as kind as they say, why does He permit all this poverty, disease, and squalor? How can He allow these poor people to be addicted to drugs and other character-destroying habits?" The minister was silent until they met a man who was especially unkempt and filthy. His hair hung down his neck and a half-inch of stubble covered his face. Then the preacher gave his response. "You can't be a very good barber, or you wouldn't permit a man like that to continue living in this neighborhood without a haircut and a shave." The atheist answered indignantly, "Why blame me for that man's condition? I can't help it if he's like that. He's never given me a chance! If he would only come to my shop, I could fix him up and make him look like a gentleman!" Giving the barber a penetrating look, the minister said, "Then don't blame God for allowing these people to continue in their evil ways when He is constantly inviting them to come and be saved. The reason they are slaves to sin and evil habits is that they refuse to accept the One who died to save and deliver them." The barber saw the point.

> *They shall not dwell in thy land, lest they make thee sin against Me; for if thou serve their gods, it will surely be a snare unto thee.*   Exodus 23:33

While a man was traveling in Jamaica, he noticed a curious shrub growing near the roadside. His companion informed him that the island people called it the "wait a bit" bush. When he inspected it closely, his clothes touched it, and he found himself snared by thorns that resembled fishhooks. The more he tried to free himself, the more he became entangled by its barbs. Finally he had to rely on his friend to release him from his hopeless situation. When you get too close to sin, you're bound to get caught.

For Further Study: Deuteronomy 7:25,26; 2 Samuel 24:10; Psalm 19:12; Jeremiah 5:25; Jeremiah 17:9; John 8:34; Romans 5:12-21; 1 John 1:9.

Sowing and Reaping

> *Be not deceived, God is not mocked, for whatever a man soweth, that shall he also reap.*   Galatians 6:7

An elderly rich man had deeded all his property to his only son and planned to live with him the rest of his life. But after a while, the daughter-in-law got tired of having him around and told her husband his father would have to leave. The son was unwilling to part with the wealth he'd received, so he decided to put his dad into the cheapest nursing home he could find. About a week later, the two men walked slowly down the road to the place where the elderly gentleman was to live. When they stopped to rest for a moment, the father began to weep. The son's conscience started to bother him, so he made some weak excuses for what he was doing. Finally, the rejected man controlled himself enough to say, "Son, I'm not crying because you're sending me to this rundown old home for senior citizens. I'm crying because of my own sins. Forty years ago I walked down this same road with my father and took him to this same place. I am only reaping what I sowed!"

Cast thy bread upon the waters; for thou shalt find it after many days.   *Ecclesiastes 11:1*

During the Civil War a man on horseback was confronted by a sentry who demanded at gunpoint that he give the password. "Lincoln," he confidently replied. A dead silence followed, for it wasn't the right word! Finally the soldier solemnly said, "If I hadn't recognized you, I would have shot you because of your mistake. At the risk of my own life I'm sparing yours. Go back and get the right word." Thanking the soldier warmly, the man rode away. When he returned, he said, "Massachusetts." "That's right, you may now pass," the guard replied. "I will not pass until I've given you a message. At the risk of your life you spared mine, so I must ask you if you have the right password for heaven." "Yes, I do!" said the sentry. "What is it?" "Jesus Christ." "Where did you learn that?" asked the man. "In your Sunday school class long ago in Pennsylvania. You planted the seed of God's Word in my life, and although you didn't know it at the time, it bore fruit. So even though you didn't have the right password, I knew you were an honest man. That's why I gave you a second chance."

He made a pit, and digged it, and is fallen into the ditch which he made.   *Psalm 7:15*

In Colorado, several people begged a trucker to free the CB channel so that they could put through an emergency call, but he refused to cooperate. They wanted to direct a doctor to the scene of a serious accident. An automobile had driven into the rear of a flatbed trailer carrying metal tubing. A piece of pipe had gone through the car's windshield, pinning a woman in the wreckage. The trucker stubbornly continued to tie up the channel, frustrating all attempts to obtain help. Then he came upon the scene of the accident, and to his utter dismay he discovered that the critically injured person was his own wife! When a doctor finally did arrive, he said that if he had been notified even 10 minutes earlier the woman's chances for survival would have been much greater.

His mischief shall return upon his own head, and his violent dealing shall come down upon his own pate.   Psalm 7:16

The eighth-century emperor Charlemagne wanted to have a magnificent bell cast for the church he had built. An artist named Tancho was employed to make it. He was furnished, at his own request, with a great quantity of copper and a hundred pounds of silver for the purpose. He kept the silver for his own personal use, however, and used highly purified tin instead. When the work was completed, he presented the bell to the Emperor, who had it suspended in the church tower. But the people were unable to ring it. So Tancho himself was called in to help. He pulled so hard to make it ring that its clapper fell down and killed him.

For Further Study: Psalm 126:5,6; Proverbs 11:18,19; Proverbs 22:8; Hosea 8:5-14; Hosea 10:12.

Success/Failure

This book of the law shall not depart out of thy mouth, but thou shalt meditate therein day and night, that thou mayest observe to do according to all that is written therein; for then thou shalt make thy way prosperous, and then thou shalt have good success.   Joshua 1:8

A young teen named John W. Yates was so poor that he had to put cardboard in his shoes to cover up the holes. When he opened a bank account at the age of 15, however, he deposited his meager earnings under the name "John W. Yates and Company." By this he was indicating that God was his partner and manager, and he followed that practice throughout his life. In time he became a multimillionaire.

Another young man, Oswald Chambers of Scotland, showed so much artistic promise that at the age of 18 he was invited to study under Europe's greatest masters. But he declined the offer and enrolled in a little-known Bible school, where he eventually became a teacher. Later, he went to Egypt and ministered to the spiritual needs of British soldiers. Chambers died there when he was only in his forties, but he left to the world a rich legacy of devotional literature. For both men, doing God's will was their prime objective; both were a success.

And Jesus said unto him, No man, having put his hand to the plough, and looking back, is fit for the kingdom of God.   Luke 9:62

Many people have become very successful after an initial experience of failure because they didn't let it defeat them. Nathaniel Hawthorne, for example, lost his position in the customhouse at Salem, Massachusetts. Feeling very low, he told his wife the bad news, expecting her to share his dismay. But to his surprise she responded with delight. "Now you can continue work on your book." With her encouragement he got busy and finished *The Scarlet Letter,* which literary critics say is one of the finest novels ever written in the United States.

Phillips Brooks failed miserably as a teacher, but he later went on to achieve great prominence. When he sensed that he was not cut out to be a teacher, he decided to prepare himself for the ministry. He was an outstanding success, and his name appears in lists of the best-known American clergymen.

Brethren, I count not myself to have apprehended;
but this one thing I do, forgetting those things which
are behind, and reaching forth unto those things
which are before, I press toward the mark for the
prize of the high calling of God in Christ Jesus.
                                    Philippians 3:13,14

About 400 years before Christ, a gifted Greek named Timanthes took instruction in art from a well-known tutor. After several years the budding young painter created an exquisite picture. When he was commended for his accomplishment, he became so enraptured with what he had produced that he sat day after day just gazing at it. He mistakenly believed he would never be able to advance beyond that point. One morning when he went to admire his work again, he discovered that the master had blotted it out. Angry and in tears, Timanthes ran to him and asked why he had destroyed his cherished possession. The wise man replied, "I did it for your own good. That painting was retarding your progress. While it was an excellent piece of art, it was not perfect—even though it appeared that way to you. Start again and see if you can do even better!" The student took his advice and produced his masterpiece called *Sacrifice of Iphigenia,* which is regarded as one of the finest paintings of all antiquity.

My brethren, count it all joy when ye fall into
various trials, knowing this, that the testing of your
faith worketh patience. But let patience have her
perfect work, that ye may be perfect and entire,
lacking nothing.   *James 1:2-4*

Many years ago a gifted young man in London began preparing for the ministry. He had surrendered his life to Christ, and he wanted to be used by the Lord. He was a brilliant student and completed his studies at the seminary with honors. Prior to his ordination, he was required to preach a trial sermon before a select group of clergymen. The tenseness of the situation made him nervous, especially when he saw his beautiful fiancee in the audience. In his anxiety he lost his train of thought, and the group failed to approve him for the ministry. His rejection by the examining board was a bitter disappointment, and his grief was increased when the young lady broke their engagement because he had done so poorly. He fought a terrible battle with depression. After pouring out his complaint before God, he felt the burden lifted as he realized that the Lord was working out a plan for his life. He was deeply impressed with Romans 8:28 and experienced peace in his soul. He asked to take the test again, and this time he was ordained to the ministry. The profound preaching of G. Campbell Morgan was to move the masses by its biblical depth and heartwarming appeal. The renowned expositor authored several Bible commentaries and 60 books on theology. He left a legacy of sermons that still stir the hearts of people whenever they are read. The crisis he survived by God's grace helped make him a spiritual giant.

For Further Study: Romans 8:31; Romans 8:37; Galatians 6:7-9; Philippians 4:12; 1 John 4:4; 1 John 5:4.

Talents

Then he that had received the one talent came and said, Lord, I knew thee, that thou art an hard man, reaping where thou hast not sown, and gathering where thou hast not spread, and I was afraid, and went and hid thy talent in the earth; lo, there thou hast what is thine.   Matthew 25:24,25

The English artist Dante Rossetti relates this story. One day a gentleman came to his studio with samples of his drawings and requested his candid opinion concerning them. Looking them over, he saw that they had little value, and in a kindly way he told his visitor that he needed more training. The man then brought out another set of sketches and spread them before Rossetti, saying that they were the work of a young student. The master artist immediately recognized that they displayed a remarkable talent. He enthusiastically predicted that without a doubt the youth would soon distinguish himself. Then the man said regretfully, "Sir, I was that student. I failed to persevere in my work because my teacher seemed so demanding. Now I find that through the years I have slipped backward. You are right in your estimation of my latest drawings. As I feared, they are of little or no value."

I have planted, Apollos watered, but God gave the increase.   *1 Corinthians 3:6*

The great pianist Paderewski was giving a performance in Carnegie Hall. In the audience was a mother and her young son. During the intermission, the woman suddenly realized that the boy was no longer at her side. Just then, over the voices of the milling crowd she heard the distinct notes of "Chopsticks" being played on the piano. The child had wandered onto the stage and was sitting at the magnificent Steinway concert grand. A moment later lovely music could be heard. Paderewski had quietly slipped behind the youngster, placed his talented hands over the boy's, and was adding a beautiful accompaniment to that simple tune.

For Further Study: Matthew 25:14-30; Luke 12:41-48; 1 Corinthians 12; Ephesians 4:1-16; Colossians 3:23.

Temptation

Let us walk honestly, as in the day; not in reveling and drunkenness, not in immorality and wantonness, not in strife and envying. But put ye on the Lord Jesus Christ, and make not provision for the flesh, to fulfill its lusts.   *Romans 13:13,14*

Back in the horse-and-buggy days, a certain man was plagued by the drink habit. He would gain temporary victory over alcohol, but then he would succumb again to its evil appeal. Every time he fell, he would be thoroughly humiliated and resolve to "turn over a new leaf"—but it didn't last. In spite of his shameful record, he attended church regularly. Ironically, however, that was when he often stumbled. The saloon was just a block away from the sanctuary, and when he walked past the door the temptation was just too great. Finally in desperation he went to the minister for advice. "Pastor," he pleaded, "is there anything you can do to help me?" The wise old preacher was well aware of the man's problem, so he asked, "Tell me, where do you hitch your horse?" The troubled man replied, "Down the street. There's a hitching post right in front of the tavern." "Well, why don't you change your hitching post!" said the pastor. "Use the one on the other side of the church, and you won't have to walk past the place of your temptation!"

For Further Study: Romans 6:12-14; 1 Corinthians 10:13; Ephesians 6:13-17; Hebrews 4:15; James 1:13-15.

Testimony

> *Ye are our epistle, written in our hearts, known and read of all men; forasmuch as ye are manifestly declared to be the epistle of Christ ministered by us, written not with ink but with the Spirit of the living God; not in tables of stone but in fleshy tables of the heart.* 2 Corinthians 3:2,3

A minister was making a wooden trellis to support a climbing vine. As he was pounding away, he noticed that a little boy was watching him. The youngster didn't say a word, so the preacher kept working. He was sure the lad would soon leave—but he didn't. Pleased at the thought that his work was being admired, the pastor finally said, "Well, son, trying to pick up some pointers on carpentry work?" "Nope. I'm just waiting to hear what a preacher says when he hits his thumb with a hammer."

*But, beloved, we are persuaded better things of you,
and things that accompany salvation, though we
thus speak. For God is not unrighteous to forget
your work and labor of love, which ye have shown
toward His name, in that ye have ministered to the
saints, and do minister.*   Hebrews 6:9,10

The story is told about a man who claimed that he "got religion." An old crony who knew about his shameful past heard the news, called him on the phone, and said, "Joe, they tell me you've got religion." "I sure have," came the reply. His friend responded, "Then I suppose you'll be going to church every Sunday." "That's right," Joe affirmed, "I started 5 weeks ago and haven't missed a service since." "And I suppose you're going to quit smoking and drinking." "Already have," Joe replied. "In fact, I haven't smoked a cigarette or touched a drop of liquor since." His friend paused for a moment. Finally, remembering that Joe owed him money, he said with an intended jab, "I suppose too, now that you've got religion, you're going to pay up all your old debts." At that point Joe exploded and exclaimed, "Now wait a minute! That's not religion you're talking about; that's business!"

*For we who live are always delivered unto death for
Jesus' sake, that the life also of Jesus might be
made manifest in our mortal flesh.*
                              2 Corinthians 4:11

A Jewish woman had been converted. The friend who led her to the Lord suggested that she begin her Bible reading with the gospels. She did this with great delight, and she received much spiritual benefit. But when she was finished, she told her friend she wanted to read a book on church history. Asked why she was so interested in that subject, she replied, "Oh, I'm just curious. I've been wondering when it was that Christians started to become so unlike Christ."

*Moreover, he must have a good report of them who
are outside, lest he fall into reproach and the snare
of the devil.* 1 Timothy 3:7

The Christian walk of Will Houghton, a preacher who became the president of Moody Bible Institute during the 1940s, played a large role in the conversion of an agnostic who was contemplating suicide. The skeptic was desperate, but he decided that if he could find a minister who lived his faith he would listen to him. So he hired a private detective to watch Houghton. When the investigator's report came back, it revealed that this preacher's life was above reproach. He was for real! The agnostic went to Houghton's church, accepted Christ, and later sent his daughter to Moody Bible Institute.

*Blessed are the people that know the joyful sound;
they shall walk, O Lord, in the light of Thy
countenance. In Thy name shall they rejoice all the
day; and in Thy righteousness shall they be
exalted.* Psalm 89:15,16

Many years ago some men were prospecting for gold in Montana, and one of them found an unusual stone. When he broke it open, he was excited to see that it contained gold. Working eagerly, the men soon discovered a rich vein of gold ore. Happily, they began shouting with delight, "We've found it! We've found gold! We're rich!" They had to interrupt their celebrating, though, to go into a nearby town and stock up on supplies. Before they left camp, the men agreed not to tell a soul about their find. Indeed, no one breathed a word about it to anyone while they were in town. Much to their dismay, however, when they were about to return, hundreds of men were prepared to follow them. When they asked the crowd to tell who "squealed," the reply came, "No one had to. Your faces showed it!"

But thou shalt have a perfect and just weight; a
perfect and just measure shalt thou have, that thy
days may be lengthened in the land which the Lord
thy God giveth thee. For all who do such things, and
all who do unrighteously, are an abomination unto
the Lord thy God.   *Deuteronomy 25:15,16*

In a certain village a man who sold wood to his neighbors always took advantage of them by cutting his logs a few inches under the required 4 feet. One day the report was circulated that the woodchopper had been converted. Nobody believed it, for they all declared that he was beyond being reached. One man, however, slipped quietly out of the grocery store where the conversion was being discussed. He soon came running back in excitement and shouted: "It's true! He has been converted!" They all asked, "How do you know?" "Well, I measured the wood he cut yesterday, and it's a good 4 feet long!" That convinced the crowd. The woodcutter's changed behavior revealed a changed life.

Blessed are ye, when men shall hate you, and when
they shall separate you from their company, and
shall reproach you, and cast out your name as evil,
for the Son of man's sake.   *Luke 6:22*

While conducting meetings for a Highland regiment in Egypt, Stuart Holden became acquainted with a big sergeant who was a shining, effervescent Christian. Holden asked him how he had been brought to the Savior, and the soldier told about his conversion. "There is a private in this company," he said, "who was converted in Malta before the regiment came to Egypt. We gave that fellow an awful time. One terrible night he came in very tired and wet. But before getting into bed, he knelt down to pray. My boots were soaked with water and covered with mud, and I let him have it with one on the side of his head, and struck him with the second on the other side. But he just went on praying.

The next morning I found those boots beautifully polished and standing by the side of my bed. That was his reply to me, and it broke my heart. That day I accepted his Savior as mine."

Therefore, I endure all things for the elect's sake, that they may also obtain the salvation which is in Christ Jesus with eternal glory.   2 Timothy 2:10

Pastor Stanley Dean told this story: "An unconverted man whose pretty 3-year-old daughter was seriously ill came to see me. 'Mr. Dean,' he said, 'will you come home with me? I need your help, for I just don't know how my wife will take it if our little girl dies.' When we arrived, the doctor looked at me and shook his head. Shortly afterward, the child slipped away to be with the Lord. The father began to cry, and with a scream he ran out of the house. I spoke a few words of comfort to the mother and then stepped out to find him. He was standing in the yard wringing his hands while the tears streamed down his cheeks. 'I don't know how my wife is going to take it!' he said. 'Your wife will be all right; she has One to comfort her. We're concerned about you,' I replied. When we went back into the house, we found his wife kneeling beside the child's crib. Amid sobs she was praising the Lord for the joy she had experienced for 3 years with her little daughter. The heartbroken father walked over to his wife and said, 'Honey, if God can help you in an hour like this, I want to know Him too.' Her words and actions had shown him the reality of her faith, and he was gloriously saved."

Be not thou, therefore, ashamed of the testimony of our Lord, nor of me His prisoner; but be thou partaker of the afflictions of the gospel according to the power of God.   2 Timothy 1:8

Evangelist Billy Sunday used to tell a story of a professing Christian who got a job in a lumber camp that had the reputation of being very ungodly. When a friend heard that he had been hired, he said to him, "If those lumberjacks ever find out you're a Christian, you're going to be in for a hard time!" The man responded, "I know it, but I really need the job!" After he had been working at the camp for a year, he met the friend who had predicted the ridicule and persecution he would receive from the other lumberjacks. "Well, how did it go?" asked the friend. "Did they give you a hard time because you're a Christian?" "Oh, no, not at all," the man replied. "They didn't give me a bit of trouble—they never even found out!"

Whosoever, therefore, shall confess Me before men, him will I confess also before My Father.
Matthew 10:32

At the close of a meeting being conducted by D. L. Moody, a little Norwegian boy went forward to testify of his faith in the Lord. He had difficulty speaking English, yet he wanted the congregation to know that he had been saved and that he loved Jesus. The youngster stood at the front for a moment without speaking, and he trembled as the tears trickled down his cheeks. Finally he stammered, "I'm up here because Jesus wants me to be a witness. He promised that if I tell the world about Him, He'd tell the Father about me!" That's all he managed to say, but in those two sentences he actually communicated more than several others who were glib of tongue. Moody remarked, "That boy's testimony went straight to the heart of everyone present. 'If I tell the world.' Yes, that's exactly what the Bible means when it says we must confess Christ!"

For Further Study: Psalm 22:22; Psalm 30:1-6; Galatians 2:20; Philippians 4:9; 2 Timothy 1:12; 1 John 1:1-4.

Thankfulness/Praise

In everything give thanks; for this is the will of God in Christ Jesus concerning you.

1 Thessalonians 5:18

The following story appeared in the autobiography of Clarence E. Macartney: As two men were walking through a field, they spotted an enraged bull. Instantly they darted toward the nearest fence. The storming bull followed in hot pursuit, and it was soon apparent they wouldn't make it. Terrified, one shouted to the other, "Put up a prayer, John. We're in for it!" John answered, "I can't. I've never made a public prayer in my life." "But you must!" implored his companion. "The bull is catching up to us." "All right," panted John, "I'll say the only prayer I know. My father used to repeat it at the table: 'O Lord, for what we are about to receive, make us truly thankful.' " This humorous story suggests a valuable truth. No matter how severe the trial, Christians should give thanks in everything.

I will bless the Lord at all times; His praise shall continually be in my mouth.   *Psalm 34:1*

The enthusiastic evangelist Billy Bray went to an auction with the hope of buying an old cupboard for 6 shillings—all the money he had. He intended to use it as a pulpit in his little chapel. Although it was sold to someone else, Billy walked home cheerfully, praising the Lord. A little later the neighbor who had bought the cupboard told him he couldn't get it through the narrow doorway of his home. So he let Billy have it for the original bid of 6 shillings, even though he had paid more for it. In fact, he was so glad to be rid of it that he delivered it to the chapel free of charge. The evangelist thanked God again for his earlier disappointment, for through it a problem was solved that he had overlooked—the cartage fee.

*Praise ye the Lord. I will praise the Lord with my
whole heart.*   *Psalm 111:1*

Billy Bray was saved from a terrible life of drunkenness and sin. After his conversion he experienced one trouble after another, but he never ceased praising the Lord. At last he came to the place where all he had to eat was a dish of very small potatoes, which a friend had given him. Billy had bowed his head to offer thanks when he thought to himself: How can you thank God for such small potatoes? But Billy replied, "Go away, devil—when I was serving you, I had no potatoes at all!" Yes, praise the Lord—even for small potatoes!

*I thank Christ Jesus, our Lord, who hath enabled
me, in that He counted me faithful, putting me into
the ministry.*   *1 Timothy 1:12*

In the early 1900s, a policeman was walking his beat in Chicago when he observed a man standing before a little mission. His hat was in his hand, and the officer thought he was acting rather strange. Thinking the man might be drunk or ill, the policeman approached him. He noticed that his eyes were closed, so he nudged him and said, "What's the matter, Mac? Sick?" The man looked up and smiled. "No, sir. My name is Billy Sunday. I was converted right here in this mission. I never pass this way without taking the opportunity, if possible, to stand quietly for a moment and whisper a prayer of thanksgiving." The officer grinned understandingly. Giving the evangelist's hand a hearty grip, he said warmly, "Put 'er there, Bill! I've heard a lot about you! Keep right on with your prayer, and I'll see that no one bothers you."

For Further Study: Psalm 68:19; Psalm 92:1-3; Psalm 100; Philippians 4:6; Hebrews 13:15.

Time

See, then, that ye walk circumspectly, not as fools
but as wise, redeeming the time, because the days
are evil.   *Ephesians 5:15,16*

Someone has calculated a schedule that compares
the average lifetime with a single day, beginning at 7
in the morning.

If your age is 15, the time is 10:25 a.m.
If your age is 25, the time is 12:42 p.m.
If your age is 35, the time is 3:00 p.m.
If your age is 45, the time is 5:16 p.m.
If your age is 55, the time is 7:34 p.m.
If your age is 65, the time is 9:55 p.m.
If your age is 70, the time is 11:00 p.m.
What time is it for you?

So teach us to number our days, that we may apply
our hearts unto wisdom.   *Psalm 90:12*

John Erskine, the well-known author and lecturer,
said that he learned the most valuable lesson of his life
when he was 14 years old. His piano teacher asked him
how much he practiced each day. He replied that he
usually sat down for an hour or more. "Oh, don't do
that," warned the instructor. "When you grow up, time
won't come to you in long stretches like that. Do your
practicing in minutes wherever you can find them — 5
or 10 before school, a few after lunch or in between
chores. Spread it throughout the day, and music will
become a part of your life." Erskine said that he later
applied this principle to his writing. He wrote nearly
all of his most famous work, *The Private Life of Helen
of Troy,* on streetcars while commuting between his
home and the university.

For Further Study: Psalm 39:4; Ecclesiastes 12:1-7;
John 9:4; John 12:35; 2 Corinthians 6:1,2.

Tongue

Thou shalt not take the name of the Lord thy God in vain; for the Lord will not hold him guiltless that taketh His name in vain.   *Exodus 20:7*

A godly farmer was attending a meeting of an agricultural society. Some of the men were freely using the words "devil" and "hell." He felt uneasy but said nothing. Then someone said, "Jesus Christ!" Immediately the farmer spoke up. "Sir, you may speak lightly of *your* master, but when you take *my* Master's name in vain, I object. Talk about your master, the devil, if you want to, but please leave my Lord out of it."

Death and life are in the power of the tongue, and they that love it shall eat the fruit thereof.
    Proverbs 18:21

The story is told by Franklin Allee about a family living in a small town in North Dakota. The mother had not been well since the birth of her second baby, but everyone knew that she did all she could to create an atmosphere of love in that home. The neighbors would see the father being met at the door each night with hugs and kisses from his wife and two small children. In the summer they could hear the laughter and joyous good fun coming from within the house. Often the family would romp together in the backyard while the mother looked on, thoroughly enjoying their activity. Then one day a village gossip whispered that the man was being unfaithful to his wife—a story entirely without foundation. Eventually it came to her ears, and it was more than she could bear. A few weeks later she suffered a mental collapse, and one evening when her husband came home no one met him. There was a coldness and quietness that sent a chill of fear over his heart. Soon the awful truth became apparent. He found that his wife, sick and in despair, had taken the lives of her two children before committing suicide.

The man was beside himself with grief. Later his innocence was proven to all, but the gossip's tongue had already borne its terrible fruit.

A talebearer revealeth secrets, but he that is of a faithful spirit concealeth the matter.

Proverbs 11:13

A woman repeated a bit of gossip about a neighbor, and within a short time the whole town had heard it. The person it concerned was deeply hurt and distressed. Then one day the lady responsible for spreading the rumor learned that it was completely untrue. She was sorry for what she had done and went to a wise old sage to find out what she could do to repair the damage. After listening to her problem, he said, "Go to the marketplace, purchase a fowl, and have it killed. Then on your way home pluck its feathers one by one and drop them along the path." Although she was surprised by this unusual advice, the woman did as she was told. The next day she returned and informed the man that she had done as he instructed. "Now go and collect all those feathers and bring them back to me," he said. The lady followed the same path, but to her dismay the wind had blown all the feathers away. After searching all day long, she returned with only two or three in her hand—all that could be found. "You see," said the old gentleman, "it's easy to drop them, but impossible to bring them all back. So it is with gossip. It doesn't take much to spread a false rumor, but you can never completely undo the wrong."

Judge not, that ye be not judged. For with what judgment ye judge, ye shall be judged; and with what measure ye measure, it shall be measured to you again.

Matthew 7:1,2

John Wesley was deeply disturbed by people who seemed to enjoy criticizing others, especially those in the Lord's work. Once while he was preaching, he noticed a lady in the audience who was known for her critical attitude. All through the service she stared at his new tie. When the meeting ended, she came up to him and said sharply, "Mr. Wesley, the strings on your bow tie are much too long. It's an offense to me!" He asked if any of the ladies present happened to have a pair of scissors in their purse. When they were handed to him, he gave them to his critic and asked her to trim the streamers to her liking. After she clipped them off near the collar, he said, "Are you sure they're all right now?" "Yes, that's much better." "Then let me have those shears a moment," said Wesley. "I'm sure you wouldn't mind if I also gave you a bit of correction. I don't want to be cruel, but I must tell you, madam, that your tongue is an offense to me—it's too long! Please stick it out. I'd like to take some off." Wesley didn't go through with his threat, of course, but he had made his point.

Let us not, therefore, judge one another anymore; but judge this, rather: that no man put a stumbling block or an occasion to fall in his brother's way.
Romans 14:13

DeWitt Talmage remarked, "Without exception, the people who have the greatest number of faults are themselves the most merciless in their criticism of others. They spend their lives looking for something lowly rather than something lofty." A preacher, capitalizing on this fact, devised an effective way of handling such critics. He kept a special book labeled, "Complaints of Members Against One Another." When one of them would tell him about some fault of a fellow parishioner, he would say, "Well, here's my complaint book. I'll write down what you say, and you can sign your name to it. When I see that person, I'll take up the matter with him." That open ledger, and the critic's awareness of his own faults, always had a restraining effect. Immediately the complainer would exclaim, "Oh, no, I couldn't sign anything like that!" In 40 years that book was opened a thousand times, but no entry was ever made.

Let your speech be always with grace, seasoned
with salt, that ye know how ye ought to answer every
man.   *Colossians 4:6*

A woman developed a very serious throat condition. The doctor prescribed medication but he told her that her vocal cords needed total rest—no talking for 6 months! With a husband and six children to care for, it seemed an impossible order, but she cooperated. When she needed the youngsters, she blew a whistle. Instructions became written memos, and questions were answered on pads of paper she had placed around the house. The 6 months passed, and after she recovered, her first comments were quite revealing. She said that the children had become quieter, and then she remarked, "I don't think I'll ever holler again like I used to." When asked about the notes, she replied, "You'd be surprised how many hastily written notes I crumpled up and threw into the wastebasket before I gave them to anyone to read. Seeing my own words that I would have spoken had an effect that I don't think I can ever forget."

If any man among you seem to be religious, and
bridleth not his tongue, but deceiveth his own heart,
this man's religion is vain.   *James 1:26*

On June 9, 1742, John Wesley made an interesting entry in his journal. He told of riding to a neighboring town to wait for a justice of the peace, whom he called "a man of candor and understanding." The magistrate was to hear the complaints of some angry citizens who had brought to him "a whole wagonload of these new heretics"—probably some of Wesley's converts. When the justice asked what they had done, one of the accusers replied, "Why, they pretended to be better than other people; and besides, they prayed from morning to night." "But have they done nothing else?" "Yes, sir," said an old man. "They have converted my wife. Till she went among them, she had such a sharp tongue! And now she is as quiet as a lamb." "Carry them back, carry them back," replied the justice, "and let them convert all the scolds in town."

Where no wood is, there the fire goeth out; so where there is no talebearer, the strife ceaseth.
Proverbs 26:20

After a minister preached a sermon on spiritual gifts, he was greeted at the door by a lady who said, "Pastor, I believe I have the gift of criticism." He looked at her and asked, "Remember the person in Jesus' parable who had the one talent? Do you recall what he did with it?" "Yes," replied the lady, "he went out and buried it." With a smile, the pastor suggested, "Go thou, and do likewise!"

For Further Study: Leviticus 19:16; Proverbs 6:12-14; Proverbs 17:7; John 8:5-11; Titus 2:6-8; James 3.

Trial

It is good for me that I have been afflicted, that I might learn Thy statutes. *Psalm 119:71*

The value of hardship for believers is illustrated by the "gator aid" given to enlisted men in a Florida training camp during World War II. The daily training for these GIs included a run through an obstacle course. On the final stretch of this endurance test, they had to grab a rope and swing across a broad, shallow pool. Under the blazing southern sun the water looked so inviting to the men that it proved too great a temptation. Hot and sweaty, most of them soon developed a curious habit of making it only halfway across the pond. The practice ended, however, when an enterprising lieutenant made it the new home for a large alligator. From that day on, the recruits left the ground 15 feet from the water's edge and fell sprawling in the dust, well over on the other side.

I know thy works, and tribulation, and poverty (but thou art rich). Revelation 2:9

The Scottish pastor John Watson called on a man from his church who had suffered a heavy financial setback. Crushed by his economic losses, the man exclaimed, "Everything is gone!" Without hesitation, Watson answered, "Oh, I'm sorry to hear that your wife is dead." The man looked up in alarm and questioned, "My wife?" His minister continued, "I'm doubly grieved to hear that you have also lost your character." Watson named one valuable asset after another until the man protested, saying that he still had all the things the pastor named. "But I thought you said you lost everything!" Then, mildly rebuking him, Watson said, "Brother, come to your senses! You've lost none of the things that are worthwhile!"

Cast thy burden upon the Lord, and He shall sustain thee. Psalm 55:22

Henry Moorhouse, a noble servant of the Lord, was going through difficult circumstances. His little daughter, who was paralyzed, was sitting in her chair as he entered the house with a package for his wife. Giving his daughter a big kiss, he asked, "Where is Mother?" "Upstairs," she replied. "Well, I have something for her." "Let me carry it to Mother," said the daughter. "Why Minnie dear, how can you carry this package? You cannot carry yourself." With a big smile, the child replied, "Oh no, Papa; but if you give it to me, then I will carry the package and you can carry

160

me." God spoke softly to his heart that this was his own position. He was carrying his burden, but wasn't the Lord also carrying him?

My flesh and my heart fail, but God is the strength of my heart, and my portion forever. Psalm 73:26

Inner strength in the face of trial is illustrated by the following story about a handicapped high school student. Although the crutches on which he hobbled kept him from being physically active, he excelled in his studies and was well-liked by his peers. They saw the problems he had getting around, and they sometimes felt sorry for him, but for a long time nobody asked why he had this difficulty. One day, however, his closest friend finally did. "It was polio," answered the student. The friend responded, "With so many difficulties, how do you keep from becoming bitter?" Tapping his chest with his hand, the young man replied with a smile, "It never touched my heart."

We are troubled on every side, yet not distressed; we are perplexed, but not in despair; persecuted, but not forsaken; cast down, but not destroyed; always bearing about in the body the dying of the Lord Jesus, that the life also of Jesus might be made manifest in our body. 2 Corinthians 4:8-10

In recounting his experiences as a political prisoner in Russia, Alexander Solzhenitsyn told of a moment when he was on the verge of giving up all hope. He was forced to work 12 hours a day at hard labor while existing on a starvation diet, and he had become seriously ill. The doctors feared for his life. One afternoon, while shoveling sand under a blazing sun, he simply stopped working. He did so even though he knew the guards would beat him severely — perhaps to death. But he felt that he just couldn't go on. Then he saw another prisoner, a fellow Christian, moving cautiously toward him. Without speaking, the man drew a cross in the sand with his cane and then quickly erased it. In that brief moment, Solzhenitsyn felt all of the hope of the gospel flood through his soul. It gave him courage to endure that difficult day and the months of imprisonment that followed.

And whether we be afflicted, it is for your consolation and salvation, which is effectual in the enduring of the same sufferings which we also suffer. 2 Corinthians 1:6

When the brilliant William Moon of England was ready to embark upon a promising career, he suddenly went blind! At first he couldn't accept this trial, and he exclaimed bitterly, "What are all my abilities worth now that I am shut up here in my room and the whole world is shut out?" Slowly he began to realize that God had a wise purpose in allowing this affliction. Because his own eyes were sightless, he began to develop a unique system of reproducing the alphabet to assist others in a similar condition. It soon was adapted to fit the languages of many different countries, including remote areas of the world. Millions of blind people were thus enabled to read the Bible through this system of embossed type. In an unusual way, William Moon had become a "missionary," and had brought "consolation and salvation" to many. He could rejoice because out of his tragedy had come a great triumph.

God is our refuge and strength, a very present help in trouble. Psalm 46:1

Horatio G. Spafford, an earnest Christian lawyer from Chicago, put his wife and family on an ocean liner bound for Le Havre, France. In the mid-Atlantic the steamship collided with another vessel. Twelve minutes later it went down, carrying most of its crew and passengers with it. Among them were Mr. Spafford's four children. His wife, however, was rescued and taken to Le Havre with the other survivors. Immediate-

162

ly she cabled her husband in Chicago: "Saved—alone."
The message struck him with full force and plunged
him into deep sorrow. Some time later Spafford wrote
the gospel song that has been repeated by Christians
around the world: "When peace, like a river, attendeth
my way,/ When sorrows like sea-billows roll,/ Whatever
my lot, Thou has taught me to say,/ It is well, it is well
with my soul."

For Further Study: Psalm 27:5; Psalm 40:1,2; John 16:20;
2 Corinthians 1:3-6; 2 Corinthians 4:11-18; 1 Peter 5:10.

Worldliness

But fornication, and all uncleanness, or
covetousness, let it not be once named among you,
as becometh saints.   *Ephesians 5:3*

The story is told that a friend of Augustine named
Alypius was often urged by his neighbors to watch the
gladiators in combat. He refused to do so because he ab-
horred the brutality of those barbaric contests. One
day, however, he was forced into the amphitheater
against his will. Determined not to witness the gory
spectacle, Alypius kept his eyes tightly closed. But a
piercing cry from one of the fighters aroused his
curiosity, and he peeked just as the fatal wound was
received. J. N. Norton says of the incident, "No sooner
had Alypius discovered the bloody stream issuing from
the victim's side, than his finer sensibilities were
blunted, and he joined in the shouts and exclamations
of the noisy mob about him. From that moment he was
a changed man—changed for the worse. Not only did
he attend such sports himself, but he urged others to do
likewise."

My son, if sinners entice thee, consent thou not.
                          Proverbs 1:10

A Christian teenager was urged by his mother to
memorize certain texts from the book of Proverbs. Her

163

request had been prompted by the fact that there were alcoholics in her own family. While on a vacation cruise, this young fellow was approached by two men who were drinking hard liquor. Even though he was under-age, they said, "Come on, join us." But he rejected their invitation. Then he quoted Proverbs 20:1, "Wine is a mocker, strong drink is raging, and whosoever is deceived thereby is not wise." When they continued to insist that a glass or two wouldn't hurt him, he replied, "But Proverbs 23:32 says, 'At the last it biteth like a serpent, and stingeth like an adder.' " "Oh, don't be a sissy. Have a little," they persisted. But he steadfastly replied, "Proverbs 1:10 says, 'My son, if sinners entice thee, consent thou not.' " Finally his tempters decided he was too religious, and they left him alone. Because that young believer knew these admonitions from the Bible, he was protected from the snare of alcohol. He was wise enough to avoid the seductive "wiles of the devil."

Wine is a mocker, strong drink is raging, and whosoever is deceived thereby is not wise.

Proverbs 20:1

In his book *God Will Help Me,* Walter G. Swanson referred to the life of Robert Dollar. He wrote: "A keen-eyed young sea captain stood in the lobby of a large hotel in Hong Kong conversing with an Englishman. 'So you've come to do business in the Orient? Well, step into the bar and tell me about your plans.' 'I'm sorry,' said the seaman, 'but I never partake of alcoholic beverages.' The man's florid face broke into an unbelieving smile. 'Entering the oriental trade without having a Scotch and soda?' 'Yes, sir!' 'Do you expect to be successful without taking your friends into a tavern for a drink? If you do,' he said with a cynical laugh, 'God help you!' The young man replied, 'God WILL help me.' And he was right. Years later, Robert Dollar stood on the 10th floor of the building that bore his name near San Francisco Bay. He was watching the workmen unload cargo from his freighters that had come from all over the world. He had avoided the pitfalls of liquor, and he had indeed been richly blessed by the Lord."

Wherefore, come out from among them, and be ye separate, saith the Lord, and touch not the unclean thing; and I will receive you.   2 Corinthians 6:17

Believers who ignore the importance of separation from the world will soon lose their distinctiveness as Christians. This truth is illustrated by the following account from the book *Old Testament Anecdotes:* "The Rhone, as it issues from Lake Geneva . . . , is the most beautiful of rivers—green as an emerald, yet as clear as clearest glass. . . . The Arve—a river of about the same size, and flowing for some distance nearly parallel with the Rhone and but a little way from it—is a dirty stream, carrying with it the wash of the mountains and the mud of the valley. About two miles below Geneva these two rivers unite and flow together toward the sea. But, though joined in one channel, they are still for several miles almost as distinct as when they occupied their separate beds. . . . Some miles below the junction, the river rushes into a chasm beneath a mountain. When it issues on the farther side, it is one river—called the Rhone, but in character the [muddy] Arve."

Be sober, be vigilant, because your adversary, the devil, like a roaring lion walketh about, seeking whom he may devour.   1 Peter 5:8

In an issue of *Pulpit Helps* is a humorous tale about a hunter who had his gun aimed at a large bear and was ready to pull the trigger. Just then the bear spoke in a soft, soothing voice, saying, "Isn't it better to talk than to shoot? Why don't we negotiate the matter? What is it you want?" The hunter lowered his rifle and answered, "I would like a fur coat." "That's good," said the bear. "I think that's something we can talk about. All I want is a full stomach; maybe we can reach a compromise." So they sat down to talk it over. A little while later the bear walked away alone. The negotiations had been successful—the bear had a full stomach, and the hunter had a fur coat!

For Further Study: Romans 12:1,2; 2 Timothy 2:4; Titus 2:11-14; James 4:4; 1 Peter 2:11,12; 1 John 2:15-17.

Worry

And He said unto His disciples, Therefore, I say unto you, Be not anxious for your life, what ye shall eat; neither for the body, what ye shall put on. The life is more than food, and the body is more than raiment. Consider the ravens; for they neither sow nor reap, which neither have storehouse nor barn, and God feedeth them; how much more are ye better than the fowls?   Luke 12:22-24

According to J. Arthur Rank, there is a practical way of handling the problem of worry. Not having enough faith to overcome his troubles immediately, he decided that the next best thing was to postpone thinking about them until his mind had cleared. So when something disturbing occurred, he wrote the problem on a card and would not dwell on it until a little time had passed. Then a week or so later, when he reviewed those difficulties, he found to his surprise that most of them had already disappeared. He therefore concluded that much of his distress was an unnecessary waste of energy and loss of sleep, for God had stepped in and directed things along paths he had never envisioned.

For Further Study: Psalm 127:2; Jeremiah 17:7,8; Matthew 6:34; Luke 10:38-42; Luke 12:16-34; Philippians 4:6,7; 1 Peter 5:6,7.

Yieldedness/Submissiveness

And they came to the place which God had told him
of; and Abraham built an altar there, and laid the
wood in order, and bound Isaac, his son, and laid
him on the altar.   *Genesis 22:9*

Pastor William Sangster went into a hospital room
to visit a little girl who was losing her sight. Fear
seemed to grip the youngster as with nearly blind eyes
she turned her face toward the preacher. "Oh, Dr.
Sangster, God is taking away my sight." The loving
pastor leaned down to the frightened child and said
tenderly, "Don't let Him take it—give it to Him."

Know ye not that to whom ye yield yourselves
servants to obey, his servants ye are whom ye obey,
whether of sin unto death, or of obedience unto
righteousness?   *Romans 6:16*

In his book *The Dedicated Life,* James H. McConkey
wrote about his response to a message on dedication he
had heard in a nearby city. At the conclusion the speaker prayed, "O Lord, You know we can trust the Man
who died for us." As McConkey left the meeting, he
pondered deeply the far-reaching implications of total
surrender to Christ, and he became afraid. Immediately the words came to him, "You can trust the Man who
died for you." As he rode the train home, he thought
about the changes and sacrifices he might face, and
again he became fearful. But as before, that same
message flashed through his mind. When he got back
to his room, he fell to his knees and caught a glimpse of
his past life. He had been a Christian, an officer in the
church, and a Sunday school superintendent for years,
but he had never given himself without reservation to
the Lord. Later he wrote, "So my soul began shrinking
back. And then for the last time, with a swift rush of
convicting power, there came again to my innermost
heart that searching message: 'My child, you can trust

the Man who died for you. If you can't trust Him, whom can you trust?' That settled it for me!"

And Jacob was left alone; and there wrestled a man with him until the breaking of the day. And when he saw that he prevailed not against him, he touched the hollow of his thigh; and the hollow of Jacob's thigh was out of joint, as he wrestled with him.
              Genesis 32:24,25

Commenting to a physician friend of his, James H. McConkey said, "Doctor, what is the exact significance of God's touching Jacob upon the sinew of his thigh?" The doctor replied, "That is the strongest tissue in the human body. A horse could scarcely tear it apart." "Ah, I see," said McConkey, "God has to break us down at the strongest part of our self-life before He can have His own way of blessing with us."

And the world passeth away, and the lust of it; but he that doeth the will of God abideth forever.
              1 John 2:17

The year was 1872. The setting was a barn where a small congregation had gathered for a gospel service. A soft-spoken preacher by the name of Henry Varley was concluding a message on 1 John 2:17. Lifting his eyes to the nearby haymow where an interested young man was seated, he said with emphasis, "The world has yet to see what God can do *with, for, in,* and *through* one man who is fully consecrated to Him!" The intent listener was strangely stirred and convicted by those challenging words. "Varley means any man," he said to himself. "He is not saying he has to be educated or brilliant or anything else—just a person who is willing to be used! Well, by the Holy Spirit in me, I will be that man!" Within a few years the whole world was feeling the impact of the life of that earnest young fellow who had surrendered himself to the will of God that day while seated in a haymow. He was Dwight L. Moody.

*And he fell to the earth, and heard a voice saying
unto him, Saul, Saul, why persecutest thou Me?
And he said, Who art Thou, Lord? And the Lord
said, I am Jesus, whom thou persecutest; it is hard
for thee to kick against the goads. And he,
trembling and astonished, said, Lord, what wilt
Thou have me to do? And the Lord said unto him,
Arise, and go into the city, and it shall be told thee
what thou must do.*   *Acts 9:4-6*

At a meeting held at the famous Keswick Bible
Conference, a man stood and testified of a change in his
concept of Christ. He said, "I was a Christian before I
came to Keswick. Christ was my Savior, but I'm afraid
He was a constitutional Sovereign and I was a prime
minister. Now He is absolute Lord, and that has made
all the difference in my life! It has brought me full
blessing."

*And the king's servants said unto the king, Behold,
thy servants are ready to do whatsoever my lord,
the king, shall appoint.*   *2 Samuel 15:15*

Shortly after the Civil War, General William T.
Sherman's victorious army was scheduled to march in
a triumphal parade in a large city. On the night before,
Sherman called General Oliver O. Howard to his room
and said, "General, you were at the head of one of the
divisions that marched with me through Georgia, and
you ought rightfully to ride at the head of your division
in the parade tomorrow. But I've been asked to let the
general who preceded you in command represent the
division. I don't know what to do." General Howard
replied, "I think I am entitled to represent my division,
since I led them to victory." "Yes, you are," said
Sherman, "but I believe you are a Christian, and I was
wondering if Christian considerations might lead you
to yield your rights for the sake of peace." "Oh," said
Howard, "in that case, of course I'll yield." "All right,"
said General Sherman, "I will so arrange, and will you
please report to me in the morning at 9? You will be

riding with me at the head of the army." General Howard's willingness to submit to his commander and deny himself his rightful place led to a greater position of honor.

For Further Study: Genesis 28:20-22; Psalm 51:17; Matthew 10:38,39; Romans 6:13.

Zeal

The soul of the sluggard desireth, and hath nothing; but the soul of the diligent shall be made fat.   *Proverbs 13:4*

Employees in a Detroit business office found the following important notice on the bulletin board: "The management regrets that it has come to their attention that workers dying on the job are failing to fall down. This practice must stop, as it becomes impossible to distinguish between death and the natural movement of the staff. Any employee found dead in an upright position will be dropped from the payroll.

Therefore, seeing we have this ministry, as we have received mercy, we faint not, but have renounced the hidden things of dishonesty, not walking in craftiness, nor handling the word of God deceitfully, but by manifestation of the truth commending ourselves to every man's conscience in the sight of God.   *2 Corinthians 4:1,2*

The 17th-century English pastor Richard Baxter said he preached with great intensity because he saw himself as a dying man ministering to dying people. He always spoke as if he were preaching his last sermon and as if his listeners were hearing their last message. And what a schedule he maintained for 50 years! Each Monday and Tuesday he spent 7 hours instructing the children of his parish, not omitting even one child. On

Wednesday he went from house to house to make sure that the material needs of the widows, the aged, and the infirm were met. During the rest of the week he prepared his sermons and wrote books—a total of 160 volumes. As a result of his ministry, the town of Kidderminster was transformed. It had been a place full of sexual immorality and vice, but it became a village in which nearly every household honored God, read the Bible, and prayed. Baxter's consuming zeal had reaped a rich spiritual harvest.

For Further Study: John 2:13-17; Romans 12:9-13; 2 Corinthians 9:2; Colossians 4:12,13.

Scripture Index